D0930846

The Passion and Discipline of Strategy

The Passion and Discipline of Strategy

Krzysztof Obloj

University of Warsaw and Kozminski University, Poland

palgrave
macmillan

First published 2013 by
PALGRAVE MACMILLAN
(First Published in Polish By POLTEXT 2010)

Palgrave Macmillan in the UK is an imprint of Macmillan Publishers Limited, registered in England, company number 785998, of Houndmills, Basingstoke, Hampshire RG21 6XS.

Palgrave Macmillan in the US is a division of St Martin's Press LLC, 175 Fifth Avenue, New York, NY 10010.

Palgrave Macmillan is the global academic imprint of the above companies and has companies and representatives throughout the world.

Palgrave® and Macmillan® are registered trademarks in the United States, the United Kingdom, Europe and other countries.

ISBN 978–1–137–33493–0

This book is printed on paper suitable for recycling and made from fully managed and sustained forest sources. Logging, pulping and manufacturing processes are expected to conform to the environmental regulations of the country of origin.

A catalogue record for this book is available from the British Library.

A catalog record for this book is available from the Library of Congress.

To my sons, Jan and Tomasz

Contents

Figures

Acknowledgments

I owe much to many. I am grateful to all managers and entrepreneurs with whom I have worked during the last two decades. I am especially indebted to those who allowed me to accompany them on the long journey from the start through the development of their firms. They include Janusz Palikot, an entrepreneur, who created and put AMBRA on the path to becoming the largest producer and distributor of wines in Central Europe (he later turned to politics); Mariusz Łukasiewicz, a passionate entrepreneur, whose premature death did not prevent him from creating the innovative and successful financial institutions – Lukas Bank and Eurobank; and Grzegorz Dzik, a strategist and the CEO of Impel, the conglomerate that is a leading provider of different business services to organizations and institutions in Central Europe.

I am also pleased to acknowledge my intellectual debts to my friends and research collaborators, in particular to Garry Bruton, Mariola Ciszewska-Mlinaric, Pat Joynt, Chris Kobrak, Monika Kostera, Andrzej K. Koźmiński, Michael G. Pratt, Marc Weinstein and Aleksandra Wąsowska. They might recognize their ideas and impact in this book.

The Kozminski University and University of Warsaw Faculty of Management provided an excellent environment for teaching, research and consulting, and I am grateful to both schools for their support. During the writing of this book, I spent a considerable amount of time at the Department of Business Administration of the Sun Yat-sen Business School (SYSBS) in China. I want to express my gratitude to this institution and especially Professor Shujun Zhang, my host and research collaborator there.

The first version of this book was published in Poland by Poltext Publishers. It was originally translated by Aneta Kowalska and Cynthia Naugher-Składowski, and I owe my thanks to them. It was subsequently updated and changed for English edition, and Michael Pratt, Devanathan Sudharshan and Marc Weinstein read the manuscript and offered useful comments and suggestions for which I am very grateful.

I am grateful to the following for permission to reproduce copyright material:

A citation in Chapter 7 from R. A. Burgelman and A. S. Grove (2007) 'Let chaos reign, then rein in chaos – repeatedly: managing strategic dynamics for corporate longevity', *Strategic Management Journal* 28, p. 972. Copyright John Wiley & Sons Ltd., 2007. This material is reproduced with permission of John Wiley & Sons, Inc.

Preface

Ancient Greeks had two ways to know and make sense of reality. The first was *logos*, the way of mind, consisting of observation and analysis, which permits us to understand the surrounding world, to know its laws and to formulate pragmatic recommendations for action. When Aristotle created the formal logics and Pythagoras formulated his laws, they both followed the *logos* way.

The second way is completely different – it is *mythos*, the way of myth, ritual and common tale. When we feel passion, when what we want consumes us, when we know that it is important and makes sense, we do not seek explanations in *logos*. Of course everything can be described by biochemical reactions and selfish genes, but *logos* shows that our emotions and actions are mirrored (and maybe even born) in biological and chemical processes taking place in organisms. It might be important, but not very comforting. A more natural and important explanation for humans are rituals and stories based on experience. These things guide us through decisions and act decisively in conditions of uncertainty. Strategy is company *logos* and *mythos*. On the one hand, it is a difficult and technical discipline of environmental analysis, organizational diagnosis and creation of an effective concept of action. On the other hand, it is and should be myth, full of passion, a tale about the company's provenance, its current location and its aspirations, its identity and a tale about why it is worth devoting part of one's life to company goals.

Nowadays it is very fashionable to criticize companies, especially international corporations, and claim that they ruthlessly strive for shareholders' benefits regardless of consideration of the environment and humanity. Actually there is a myth that societal well-being requires limiting the organization's role and economic impact. Of course, the corporate world has its pathologies, but any world has them – the world of family, friends, politics or religion. Modern societies and economies need effective companies that drive innovation and generate jobs and wealth. At the same time, companies cannot exist without a functional society, which ensures public, legal, economic and cultural order – they are institutions without which businesses could not exist. Both orders – the social one and the business one – are interdependent and they build a better future on the condition that they co-exist. Together, they should build their *logos* and *mythos*.

Company strategy plays an important role in this process, bridging the external world and the future. The *logos* of strategy, that includes technical, economic and organizational activities, is supposed to help companies achieve planned results because what counts on the market is efficiency rather than methodological correctness or esthetics of strategic moves. Without efficient action everything – company, employee, supplier and customer welfare – cease to exist. But *mythos*, passion, intuition and dreams are also indispensable for the company. Mythos builds its legitimization and reputation in the outside world, as well as loyalty and commitment of people inside. It gives in the best and simplest sense of this word a meaning to the company's existence and logic of action to the market. If all companies act only rationally and in their best interests, the market becomes a soulless, technological place for exchange, and its invisible hand most often ends in the pockets of the weakest participants. When companies act strategically, a world of values, dreams and hopes appears next to the world of effectiveness. This creates the indispensable *mythos* of the company and the market – a tale not about an effective resource allocation, but about great passions and the discipline of effective strategies.

1
What Is Strategy Anyway?

At the fair of definitions and concepts

There is no single definition of strategy. There never has been nor will there ever be. Even if we allow ourselves to be more liberal methodologically and to think about ways of defining strategy other than through classical requirements using *definiendum*, we will always define strategy either too narrowly, too broadly or simply in a way that allows academics, practitioners and consultants to simultaneously agree. Does it mean that we don't understand what strategy is? No.

As a scientific discipline, strategic management is a theory of company effectiveness. It is a difficult, technical and multidisciplinary field at the intersection of modern microeconomics, financial theory, organizational studies, marketing, quantitative methods and social psychology. As a practice, strategic management is a search for the best way for companies to develop. This is why the simplest definition of strategy is a coherent and effective response to environmental challenges. Strategy is neither an elaboration of plans and budgets, nor a hundred slides in PowerPoint, nor a list of key company competencies. It is a coherent concept of action based on a few complementary key choices that allows companies to benefit from opportunities to build competitive advantage and to earn above-average results.

'Strategy', as described by Sun-Tzu in the book *Art of War* from the 6th century BC, or as discussed by 17th-century samurai Musashi Miyamoto in the *Book of Five Rings*, as in the classical treatise *About War* by Clusewitz, or as stated by Michael Porter in his famous work *Competitive Strategy*, has a different meaning but always includes common elements.[1] Also academic definitions of strategy have changed every 10 years for the last 50 years as a function of new theories and schools of strategy. Yet they include a common foundation: a set of choices made

1

by top managers using company resources and opportunities from the environment to improve effectiveness of a company's activities. Despite this common thread, strategy is even more difficult to define than it was 20 or 30 years ago. Although having a good definition of strategy is crucial for the theory and practice of management, nothing will change because in recent years the field of management has become a big market, if not to say a bazaar of theories, concepts, models and terms. There are many reasons for this.

Certainly one of the reasons is the increase in the intensity of competition, sometimes referred to as hyper-competition, globalization and faster – actual or alleged – aging of old recipes for effective management. Managers have a feeling that to fight effectively for one's place in the market, they have to seek new model solutions and new practices. Demand creates a market for theories, concepts and terms. Novelty is priceless in this market – as is the case of other products on the market. Expressiveness or even outrageousness can also be important. That is why the titles of books have become ever more radical. No one will bother with forlorn and boring titles such as *Effective Management* or *Principles of Good Management*. An optimal gambit for the launch of a new book is to signal in its title an end of strategy, structure and so on and/or to announce a new beginning (horizontal organization, virtual organization, remote working, creativity as the main company drive, China or India as the empire of the 21st century, etc.). The use of colorful metaphors, emotions and imaginative narration is universal. Typical of this is the beginning of the book by Lynda Gratton from the London Business School titled *Hot Spots*: 'You always know when you are in a Hot Spot. You feel energized and vibrantly alive. Your brain is buzzing with ideas and the people around you share your joy and excitement. The energy is palpable, bright and shining. These are times when what you and others have always known becomes clearer, when adding value becomes more possible. Times when the ideas and insights from others miraculously combine with your own in a process of synthesis from which spring novelty, new ideas and innovation. Times when you explore together what previously seemed opaque and distant.'[2]

Simultaneously many of these books and concepts incessantly repeat the same recommendations – act flexibly, quickly and stay focused. Create new markets, surprise leaders with an attack, take advantage of human resources, build organizational culture, cut expenditure, be innovative and break the rules of the game (all of them at best). It doesn't mean that these obvious claims have no sense. They are really important because, after all, management also consists of a fast, flexible, innovative action with a constant minimization of costs. The problem, however, is that there is no best way to manage or to be successful, although it is often promised by bestsellers. What is more, every novel approach gets imitated and loses with time its uniqueness and effectiveness.

A great demand for new management concepts also provokes a sort of industrialization of management schools, even those that are traditionally academic. Business schools change the logic of their functioning. The old academic centers, closed for years in ivory university towers, fight today actively for revenues as governments reduce subsidies. The simplest and often the most effective way to do this is to offer a continuing stream of new corporate training and restructure old programs such as MBAs and EMBAs. Of course, this trend is both good and bad. It brings academia closer to management practices and forces academics to pay greater attention to contemporary organizational challenges and problems. At the same time, however, it decreases the independence of thinking and changes the relationship between lecturers and students. They stop being partners for a dialog and become – which is often the case of students of MBAs and EMBAs – customers demanding recipes and instant recommendations. This forces schools (which are ever more dependent on revenues from executive management programs) to act as normal corporations, and so their curricula become products almost to the same degree as yogurt or cars.

Another reason for the growth of market-like nature of the management field is the dramatic globalization, growing professionalism and standardization of consulting services. It is a huge market worth almost 400 billion dollars, which in the 1980s grew roughly by 20 percent per year. In the last two decades, as the pace of growth decreased, consulting companies were forced (like business schools) into a more intensive fight for customers. They publish good monthly and quarterly journals (with a pinch of science) and books describing their proposals of model organizational solutions. They create new products and try to build new markets. They try above all to coin new catchy phrases, always creating additional demand. When you look carefully at the development of the consulting market, it is probably the one most driven by new ideas and phrases.[3]

In the 1970s the market was fueled with concepts and techniques of strategic planning and prognoses (e.g. Delphi, analysis of cross impacts). In the 1980s many interesting and novel ideas appeared – *kaizen*, quality circles, continuous improvement and then *reengineering*. The 1990s were less dynamic but the concept of key competences, the famous New

Economy based on the Internet and the threat of computer systems brought by the year 2000 (Y2K) added vigor to the market.

The years of the most recent decade do not have such catchy slogans and terms, which, no doubt, may also partially explain the decrease of growth dynamics of the consulting market. The convergence of such phenomena as globalization, the change of logic of business and the growing professionalism of consulting has made the management field a very competitive marketplace, in which thousands of sellers – academia, consultants, accidental prophets – try to draw the attention of managers and to think of new words and phrases which hide theories, concepts, models and solutions. Since nobody has time and the attention span, the novelty and the ability to draw attention by words alone is crucial. It is enough to look at the management market in the last years – since the word 'strategy' was an effective and interesting way to wrap any concept, everything has become strategic. Ordinary marketing has become strategic, as have human resources, logistics or finance. A price reduction has become a discount strategy; outsourcing has become a strategic concentration; concentration has become a market niche strategy; and mergers and acquisitions have become a growth strategy. What is more, the strategy field itself has started to abound in new terms and phrases, among which undoubtedly the most interesting is the *Blue ocean strategy* coined by W. Chan Kim and Renee Mauborgne, lecturers from the French business school, INSEAD.[4] It must be honestly stated that this is a more beautiful and more marketable term than 'comb analysis' or 'configuration analysis', other names of similar means to build strategy. The concept of the *Blue ocean* is also much better theoretically grounded and contains more tools than configuration analysis, which had been simply a method of designing innovative strategies or products. And as any well-wrapped product of a better quality, *Blue ocean* sells much better, until it is replaced by a new theory or concept.

Changing nature of strategy

The natural cacophony of terms, models, concepts and theories favors pessimistic voices claiming that there has been a crisis and a blur of the management field's identity. Management science and its sub-fields (such as strategic management, international management or marketing) have trouble precisely defining the scope of their research and analyses. They don't have unambiguous methodological standards, they like to use theories worked out in related fields (mainly economics and sociology), and they are vulnerable to fashion. At the same time, the management field systematically welcomes scientists from other fields – sociology, psychology and especially economics, transmitting their theories and concepts without caring too much about the existing order. The result among researchers is a constantly growing variety of discussion about the problems of management and a systematic sensation of crisis or a sense that the field is out of control. Pointless discussions and questions such as 'Is a lack of strategy a strategy?' – which is not the same as the very serious and eternal philosophical question Parmenides posed when he asked whether nonexistence is a form of existence – create an additional sense of disorder and confusion. And finally there has been a slowly growing realization that much management research has little practical value. The world of science, both in its positivistic and phenomenological version, lives its own life, with little relation to the functioning of actual organizations. Only seldom does the field realize it is time to examine real management practices.

It is worth keeping a certain distance to the immaturity of the field and to the idiosyncratic behaviors of scientists. Knowing its past and achievements helps to accomplish this. In 1995 R. Rumelt, D. Schendel and D. Teece, for all practical purposes the founding fathers of the field of strategic management, published an important collective work. It is a set of papers from a conference, which hosted the most prominent strategy theorists. Each of them had discussed precisely one key question or issue from the field. A careful study of their book reveals that there is a constant set of questions for which we have better and better answers and theoretical frameworks.[5]

In 2008 a fascinating analysis of the historical development of strategy was presented by S. Cummings and U. Daellenbach.[6] They based their analysis on 2366 articles published between 1986 and 2006 in the oldest scientific periodical of strategic management field – *Long Range Planning*. The question asked by the authors was straightforward: What was the direction of the field's evolution? The analysis showed – to the surprise of many – that a couple of terminological categories had remained almost unchanged during this period, namely corporation, organization and processes, creativity and innovativeness (this issue is not as new as authors of books discovering the meaning of company's innovativeness would like it to be), change, technology, decisions, mergers, acquisitions and disinvestments. This means that for the last 20 years the field of strategic management searches for answers to the following questions:

1) What does an organization's success depend on?
2) How are company resources organized and used?

3) How does the organization react to changes in its environment, for example, technological breakthroughs?
4) What does the process of developing a strategy look like?
5) What is the role of creativity and innovations in this process?
6) What are strategic consequences of the biggest investment decisions on mergers, acquisitions or disinvestments?

History also shows that there are terms and categories that appear out of the blue and become fashionable until their popularity starts to decrease. Such was the fate of terms such as portfolio analysis, scenario planning, vision, mission, benchmarking and the prognostic method called Delphi (who still remembers it today?), all of which had their five minutes of fame in the 1970s. In the 1990s their place was taken by terms such as organizational learning, knowledge management, organizational culture, ethics and corporate social responsibility as well as organizational networks. In addition to their historical analysis, Cummings and Daellenbach have done something very interesting – they conducted an analysis of changes in central and peripheral terms and their mutual relations. The analysis brings an important message to both practitioners and theorists, because it reveals three important trends which may well explain the amorphous boundaries of the field of strategic management.

First, central terms change – in the 1970s it was planning, in the 1980s (times of the dominance of strategy as market position) it was industry and strategy, in the 1990s it was change and strategy, and then organization, process, knowledge, relations and the adjective 'strategic' – so the substantive becomes an adjective indicating a dynamic and more systemic nature of the research and analysis.

The second trend is a growing number of terms and relations between them. Strategic management becomes a more eclectic and complex field, which reflects the real practice of building strategy in a company operating in a hyper-competitive market, which ever more often resembles the landscape during a constant earthquake.

Third, time orientation changes, which is reflected in the 'grammar' of strategy. In the 1960s and 1970s the word 'strategy' was treated as substantive and understood as a set of decisions taken today in order to build the future of an organization. The time arrow points toward the future with today as its point of departure. In the 1980s and 1990s strategy became a verb – researchers were less interested in the strategy's content and more interested in the process, in which the routines and processes shaped in the past created relatively stable patterns of actions shaping the current state and the future of the organization. Time is therefore dragged – what counts above all else is the impact of the past on the current state and the future of the company. In recent years, strategy has been ever more often treated in a complex way, as a sort of adjective. Researchers are interested in a set of strategic activities – structure, processes and relations. Time orientation changes again – researchers try to look at the company's current situation from the perspective of the future.

Regardless of how indicative the research of articles in one periodical journal is (though a 20-year period allows for an excellent overview of a field's evolution), the analysis presented shows a growing eclecticism of the field – because it reflects the changing logic of the market and the organization. Together with the growing complexity of the organization's world, the field of strategy becomes more complex, but it has its stable fundamental elements. Being enriched with new terms and models of thinking, it always tries to find its place as a link between the organization and the environment, as a flow of innovative and adaptable decisions and actions in which the past, the current state and the predictions about possible scenarios of future events play an important role. If the above analysis of strategic management's evolution allows for an explanation of the growing complexity of the field and for a discussion of theorists' uncertainty regarding its identity, it is more difficult to counter the second, more general reason for the aforementioned pessimism. It is in my opinion a natural extension of the spirit of our times, where we lack the optimism of the past. Today fear and inquietude dominate, as does the acceptance of diverse systemic imperfections of political and economic measures. Faith in the possibility of getting to know the 'true' answers by means of scientific cognition is limited. The literature is full of dramatic negative consequences of the civilization's progress, and postmodernists silently assumed as theirs the directive that 'anything goes'. The mood of the 'fashionable pessimism' has been dramatically deepened by the economic crisis that started in 2008. Its progress during 2009–11 makes us think about the words of Zorba the Greek about a 'splendiferous crash', but speaking seriously it questions the present construction of a liberal market economy with its modern concept of an organization, which has seemed to be so natural and the only right systemic measure since the decline of the alternative – the socialist system.[7]

Nobody knows now how this crisis will end, but knowing the history of economics allows us to keep a certain distance from the aforementioned pessimism. In the 20th century, we experienced at least a couple of great economic and financial crises. The crisis of the American financial system in 1907 was an endless flow of bankruptcies of financial institutions, dramatic reductions of lending capacity, price and production reduction as well as the breakdown of world stock exchanges. The stock exchange crises from 1927 and the financial crisis from 1931 were even worse. Problems of financial institutions started with the collapse of Creditanstalt, the biggest Austrian bank, and they moved to the whole of Europe (especially in Germany) and to the US in the blink of an eye. During the latter crisis, gross domestic product fell by more than 29 percent and returned to 1929 levels only in 1939! Economies almost drowned – unemployment increased, production decreased, enterprises went bankrupt and almost all major currencies devalued.

In 1971 the stable currency system created at the conference in Bretton Woods collapsed. Over the next decade, we experienced economic stagnation and a stock exchange crisis despite enormous government interventions. When it seemed that everything was all right, the great crisis of American financial institutions, the so-called *Savings and Loans Associations Crisis*, came in 1989. Over 700 banks collapsed and the American government spent roughly 100 billion dollars to save the financial sector. In 1998 a short financial crisis came, provoked by the collapse of the Long-Term Capital Management Fund. It was a fund managed by two Nobel Prize winners in economics, who had tried above all to earn a lot of money on the arbitration of marginal price differences, especially on the market of bonds, using complicated econometric models and borrowed money. Everything was all right until the Russian market collapsed and the differences were no longer marginal. The fund disappeared and the money disappeared along with it. Then a breakdown of Asian markets followed and then later a breakdown of the stock exchange performance of Internet companies, which was painful but did not last long. The world moved ahead until the bankruptcy of the huge investment bank Lehman Brothers. On September 11, 2008, rating agencies announced a radical decrease in its rating status, and on September 15, after dramatic negotiations and failed attempts to find a buyer, Lehman announced its bankruptcy. A new great crisis had begun.

These events were neither new nor inevitable, as adversaries of a liberal market economy would like to make them out to be. But the pace and scale of the crisis's development seems so unprecedented that even the most prominent economists are pretty helpless in their recommendations. As Chris Kobrak, a business historian, has accurately noted, markets and financial institutions have become too big and too global compared to the capacity of local interventions. More effective national regulation is needed and perhaps it is time for international market regulations.[8] From a managers' point of view, both the cacophony of terms created by the theory and practice of management and the new great crisis pose difficult challenges and questions: What is strategy and how to build it in unfavorable conditions of uncertainty? What should be the role of the chief executive officer, the management and the supervisory board in this process? Defining and understanding the core of strategy, its creation and realization, which are not easy in good economic conditions become even more problematic in times of a genuine uncertainty, an uncertainty not even well described by dramatic and worn words such as crisis, stagnation, recession or depression. The nature of strategy likes to get hidden – both in theory and practice. This is why I suggest the need to give up the effort to find an unambiguous definition of strategy and instead recommend a focus on core and unchangeable features of a good company strategy. As R. Rumelt, a prominent expert in the field has accurately noted: 'there is nothing like a crisis to clarify the mind. In suddenly volatile and different times you must have a strategy. I don't mean most of the things people call strategy – mission statements, audacious goals, three- to five-year budget plans. I mean a real strategy'.[9] And a genuine strategy is born from a passionate idea accompanied by emotions and uncertainty.

2
Passion and Strategic Choices

Dreams and ideas

Passion is a mysterious term with a long history. Great philosophers and scientists have deliberated on its nature because it is present in every great cultural myth, in every great story. While we may view passion as a positive feature of visionaries and innovators, historically, it has often taken a secondary role to cooler intellect. Thus, Plato saw reason as the chariot driver having to control good and bad passions. However, passion today is seen as largely unambiguously positive, especially by students of entrepreneurship. According to research it is related to pursuit of stretched goals, strong will, courage, perseverance, high level of initiative and willingness to work long hours.[1] It results from engagement in something that is extremely meaningful and this sentiment is beautifully expressed by Sunil Kant Munjal, a manager of an Indian motorcycle producer, Hero: 'If you are not passionate about a business, there is no use doing it. That's almost a philosophy for us – we will only [get involved in] businesses that have certain attributes. One is that they need to allow us to get into a significant leadership position in a reasonable timeframe. Two, we only do businesses that have a positive social impact; that is an essential requirement for us as a group, as a family, as individuals. And three, we like to do businesses that we enjoy. If you like what you do, you do not have to work.'[2]

Passion is an important ingredient of a good strategy process, and therefore it is equally useful and needed for entrepreneurs and managers. In order to clarify its impact and role I would like to start with what it is, and then discuss what it does. I propose that it focuses strategic thinking on one major orientation – change. Finally, I would like

10

to show how experience, a holistic view and imagination shape passion and the strategic choices that follow.

The simplest and most powerful definition of passion was offered a long time ago by Weber. He stated that passion is a *devotion to an object of activity for its own sake*.[3] It is the love of the game, the thrill of the hunt and the mad pursuit of an idea.

Passion seems to do two things for business people: it motivates and it binds. That is, it is what gets us moving toward a goal and it keeps us on that goal. Passion is necessary for entrepreneurs when they start from zero, but it is also a necessary element for managers to develop winning strategies of existing companies. In both cases passion means a readiness to challenge the market by undertaking an attack on the market leader, offering a revolutionary product, re-segmenting market or creating a new market, building a new business model or growing and developing a firm. The goal for a passionate business leader may take the form of a vision – a dreamed for but unrealized future.

Such a vision can take in practice different forms that can be positioned on a continuum anchored with strategic innovation on one end, a business concept or model in the middle, and focus on firm's development on the other end. It is consistent with the theory of organizational passion that suggests three types of role identities that create this continuum: an inventor identity, founder identity and developer identity.[4]

Strategists aiming for innovation focus mainly on radical change, on 'changing the world'. They experience passion when they challenge and change how we think and do things by radically altering competitive landscape. Strategists aiming for founding a business model concentrate on acquisition and configuration of resources, typically in the early stages of a venture's life cycle. They passionately exploit opportunities and grow their new ventures – be it new firms, product lines or markets. Strategists aiming for development are also passionate but more conservative in their risk appetite than change-seekers. They focus on activities related to market development (e.g. attracting new customers), and a firm's growth (e.g. via new versions of the product, new market entry, acquisitions and mergers).

In real life, when strategy becomes a practice, the distinction between innovation, establishment of business model and development is often blurred. Many entrepreneurs after establishing their ventures engage in activities related to customers and market, and focus relentlessly on their firm's growth and development. Also there are managers with a passion for innovation and change that are willing to bet the future of firms they manage onto uncertain and innovative projects. Therefore the distinction between passion for innovation and passion for development in real life is neither simple nor clear cut. It just indicates possible ends of 'passion for what' continuum. A common denominator of all possible options on this continuum is potential for change.

An extreme version of change dream of many entrepreneurs and strategists is a search for a Genuine Innovation – a creation of a new market reality. It is a way which has a nature of an unknown trail: always attractive, but difficult and risky. It is also a way which is closer to art than science. It is because its result is really an equally atypical event as the creation of impressionism or fauvism in art – a genuine innovation. Atypical doesn't necessarily mean rare. We have recently noticed that atypical events actually occur quite often. It sounds paradoxical, but the dominating normal distribution simply does not adequately describe the probability of events such as innovations – tails are fatter than we have traditionally thought. Since we don't have satisfactory probability estimates of their occurrence, we rely on the metaphor of an unusually rare event, or an estimate based on other type of events. Innovations being a result of entrepreneurs' and managers' passion, like disasters or lucky events, are single occurrences and science does not have much to say about them, even less predict them.

Innovations usually have a form of new, interesting products (e.g. Rubik's dice, Concorde plane, Segway vehicle, Belvedere vodka or Sony SmartWatch), but sometimes they give birth to whole new industries, markets or business models. This was the case in the creation and launch of MTV by the British group, Virgin and the development of an integrated production system eCMMS (e-enabled Components, Modules, Moves and Services) by Foxconn (world's biggest producer of electronic components and products). Today, when we think about an innovative company the most natural example is Apple that innovated the music market. Before iPod and iTunes development, a group of people had assessed the possibility of sending music over the Internet (Napster, Kazaa and many other peer-to-peer websites already existed and Internet users exchanged music files). The advance in technology of MP3 players and the absolute inertia and defensive attitudes of main market players created the opening. A group of Apple employees have decided that such a combination of changes and technology, together with the resources and competencies of Apple in the area of innovative products' design, created a chance to change the logic of this market's functioning. They asked why not? It turned out they were right. It was not an entirely revolutionary innovation but they created a new combination of already existing things. The passion of Steve Jobs and his co-workers at Apple permitted them to notice an opportunity to change the reality, formulate a concept for action, build products and services and introduce them with tremendous success in the market.[5] And thanks to products such as iPod, iPhone and iPad, the world changed, and at this moment Apple Computers stopped being mainly a computer producer and subsequently changed its name from Apple Computers to Apple.

The only problem with strategic passion for innovation is that unprecedented trails usually finish badly for pioneers; only a few happily reach the end. Indirect evidence of this is that almost all books on innovative companies (and there are many of those) have been written about the very same companies! We always recall and restudy the case of IKEA, Apple, 3M, Microsoft, Intel, Southwest Airlines and Ryanair, Nokia (until recently!), Toyota, Virgin, Starbucks' or Oticon.[6] It is better not to speak about other most innovative companies of the beginning of the 1990s (favorites of the American management bestsellers) because many of them have either disappeared after the Internet boom, got acquired or gone bankrupt in disgrace – for certain, partially thanks to their innovativeness.

Even the aforementioned companies which are icons of innovative strategies realize that new ideals have a shelf life. Ford and General Motors some time ago created similar revolutionary innovative strategies. It gave them great market positions in the automotive industry for many years. Ford's strategy – absolutely phenomenal, low-cost, based on one model (there was a time when the Ford T model had over 50% share on the American market!) – and Ford's excellent integrated production was beaten by General Motors' marketing segmentation strategy and its fitted divisional structure. The concept of five precisely defined market segments serviced by five decentralized but coordinated business units was a revolutionary innovation that made GM number one on the market for many years. Until another new great innovation – Toyota's business model, which was both a product of necessity and Taiichi Ohno's and Eiji Toyota's imagination. Toyota could not even try to compete with American corporations and their mass-scale business model because the Japanese market was smaller, the segmentation clearer and capital was less available. This is why it created an unusually innovative 'lean' production system, which joined flexibility, outsourcing, low costs, technological waste elimination and employee commitment to a continuous process improvement.[7] What is fascinating is probably very few managers from GM appreciate the history's irony. Toyota destroyed GM's position in exactly the same way GM had destroyed Ford's – by changing the innovative business model of the latter into weaknesses and ruining the foundation of their strategy. Thus, passion may be born out of a dream to be genuinely innovative.

A more classic dream of a strategist is Change. Its point of departure is a deep interpretation of the existing market reality and a look at the local environment of the organization in a new, different way – a way that permits us to notice phenomena and trends, most often already existing, but not obvious to everyone. The essence of change's passion is the readiness to question reality, which others take for granted. This readiness is expressed in two fundamental questions: why? and why not? People who specialize in such questions are persons with an extreme imagination or... children. Only people, who are able to notice strange or curious things in a 'normal' reality with enthusiasm, or who are able to imagine the world differently, are ready to question the world's order with questions of the 'why' type. They are able to endure through their questions or even fight for them. And fight and endurance is what they need because their dream of change appears in conditions of great uncertainty – when there is no uncertainty, there are no dreams, no passion, there are only plans in Excel sheets.

A good example of such passionate change is Nintendo Co Ltd., which has already twice in its history changed the dynamics of the computer game market. Computer games – so popular today – didn't have an easy start. When the first computers such as Commodore, Sinclair and Atari appeared, the first games and consoles appeared alongside them. Most games were boring (demanding simple manual dexterity) or too simple. Probably the biggest fiasco was a game called E.T., produced by Atari and based on the famous film by Spielberg, which was so poor that it actually provoked a crisis in the market of computer games. A small company from Japan – Nintendo – overcame this crisis. At the beginning it produced playing cards, then toys and finally in the 1980s they started to produce computer games. Nintendo made the first big market change by creating calm, almost educational adventure games for children and youth, among which Super Mario Bros and The Legend of Zelda were the most popular. In contrast to typical arcade and computer games dependent on dexterity, these games had their heroes and plots, they were good stories.

With time the market of computer games started to evolve in the direction of more spectacular, fast, adventurous games. These were the merits of technological capacities of computer consoles – first the PS2 by Sony and since 2001 also the XBox by Microsoft. Nintendo didn't have financial wherewithal to compete technologically with Sony and

Microsoft and if it hadn't been for its dominating (almost 90%) share on the world handheld consoles, it would probably have fallen out of the industry in much the same way as another traditional producer – Sega. The market for computer games has exploded but in a particular way. Games became fascinating, but more brutal, complicated and demanding in terms of the player's time, manual dexterity and memory skills. Young people have started to play ever more but children and their busy parents ever less. And Microsoft and Sony got lost in the technological and extremely expensive race to create a perfect console. In 2005 Microsoft introduced a new revolutionary console XBox 360, almost a year later Sony introduced its PS3 console and then, Nintendo introduced its Wii console, which radically changed the market. It was technologically less advanced, but elegant, simple and white, with two remote controls with motion detectors. It was enough to take the remote control and make a move with it to play tennis, golf, bowls, to box or to pilot a plane. When I first played Wii I had a feeling of going back to the 1980s. The graphics were simple, the plot almost nonexistent, and the game itself was available to anyone after a one-minute instruction. But it was at last possible to play for fun with relatives and friends – accordingly with Nintendo's vision that Wii will be a console by which people will have fun together and enjoy it together. The rest is history – by directing its console at the biggest market, the market of players who didn't play, Nintendo extended its success. All over the world people queued for a Wii and till 2008 Nintendo had sold twice as many new computer consoles as Sony and Microsoft. Two out of ten most popular games in the world, Wii Sports and Wii Fit have strength in their simplicity.[8] But as usual, the happy end was short-lived. The Nintendo face today extreme challenges – both strategic and financial (it posted financial losses in 2011 and 2012) – as casual gamers are abandoning consoles in favor of playing cheap or free games on tablets and smartphones.

In 2006 the founder of Grameen Bank, Muhammad Yunus, received the Nobel Prize. His concept of Grameen Bank's strategy, treated at the outset as a communist utopia or a smart business, deserves recognition and respect because it created a totally new business model at the intersection of a clan, a foundation and a company.[9] The program helps fight poverty and gives mainly women (almost 90% of the bank's customers) a chance to undertake economic activity. It is also a profitable business and has an absolutely phenomenal index of loan repayment – 98 percent. The logic of the bank's functioning is based on the assumption that every poor person has a right to micro loans and, in general, the bank has practically no employees but has loan committees consisting of women from villages of Bangladesh. They give loans to the poorest members of their community but on the condition that they create a five to seven-person group (a kind of a support group) from which one or two people initially receive a loan for business purposes. They repay the loan in two-week installments and after paying the whole loan other people in the group can get a loan for themselves. Since all people know each other and come from the same village – both borrowers and loan committee members – there is no need for a scoring system, formal agreement or a technical loan repayment monitoring. Tracking the way the money is used is simple and cheap. The bank also encourages its customers to join savings programs in a way to build their future financial resources. At present the bank has restructured its activities because of its size (over 7.5 million customers!), it has subsidiaries and employees, and it has widened its product range (by household loans, wireless communication, loans for education and loans for beggars with no interests), but the general logic of its strategy remains the same. Every local subsidiary acts relatively independently trying to reach goals, both financial (profit from the conducted business) and social (coming out of poverty by borrowers and financing education of children).[10] It is really important that Grameen Bank makes impact, makes money and today constitutes a widely copied model of joining business strategy and corporate social responsibility. In sum, sometimes passion stems simply from the need to be different from what is currently. To break the status quo. To change.

Passions as promise, not guarantees

It is important to note that passions motivate and bind people and companies to courses of action. This does not guarantee that the courses set, and the visions articulated, are the right way to go. For example, this was the case of Apple's hypothesis concerning the market of personal computers. In spite of a great pioneering product and in spite of creating with passion the computer market from scratch with its two products – Apple I and Apple II in the years 1976–8 – the conceptual strategy of Apple Computers was wrong from the beginning. The concept of Wozniak and Jobs assumed that a computer would be a sophisticated work tool on the market of creative industries (press, design and advertisement) and education, which both quickly turned out to be market niches.

Another conceptual mistake Apple committed was in 1993 when it launched its PDA Newton. It was probably the first product of this type on the market and it turned out to be a total failure. Only the second wave of companies that could assess technology and market requirements for such a product created an adequate market strategy at the end of the 1990s, and today thanks to the convergence of technology its function is being overtaken by smartphones. It is also worth remembering a mistake made by Microsoft. In the 1990s its passionate vision of the future was a world with a PC (equipped obviously with Windows) on every desk. It limited Microsoft's perspectives and it didn't recognize in its strategy the meaning of a community of open source software such as Linux, nor the creation of Internet and its powerful implications.

One of the most interesting strategic speculations of the 1990s was the Iridium project. A group of unusually well-educated and well-paid professionals had a dream of a world mobile communication. They assessed this market conceptually and created a basically reasonable strategy. Based on experience, imagination, limited knowledge, available technology, customer habits and investment opportunities they made important choices. The system was supposed to work globally thanks to an orbital phone network serviced by 88 satellites suspended in the low orbit (800 km) in order to ensure a fast signal transmission. The telephone was supposed to work only in open air (!) because the concept's authors thought a mobile phone would never be necessary for people closed in offices and houses – such locations had normal traditional phones after all. It was supposed to be perfect, but in its initial phase it was expensive (2000 dollars for a phone and a couple of dollars a minute) and the handset was heavy as a brick. Economies of scale and lower prices were assumed for further development. The first solemn conversation over an Iridium phone was conducted by Al Gore, the then vice president of the US, in 1998 and it was a great event but the whole concept was already a business failure. The world of mobile communication was dominated by a cheaper and simpler GSM system based on a totally different concept and a couple of months later Iridium LLC announced its bankruptcy.

It is always possible to create a coherent and intellectually interesting strategic concept – a dream, which will finally turn out to be a mistaken judgment of the future market reality. This is why every interpretation of environmental phenomena and every strategy concept should be treated like scientists treat hypotheses – we consider them to be incomplete and true only temporarily. We constantly test them by collecting new data, by discussing new opportunities, and by using imagination, we try to classify them. They are true only temporarily – until we find better concepts.

At the outset of passion there is hypothesis

The point of departure of each passionate strategy is a speculative judgment, a hypothesis that a certain coherent concept (or in other words a set of interrelated key choices concerning market, product or service, method of delivery and type of desired advantage) will allow the company to benefit from precise environmental challenges, changes and opportunities. In other words, passions have a lot in common with intuitions. They are emotional but also experiential, quick and holistic. Hence three elements are feeding passions: experience, recognition of patterns and imagination. They represent distinctive streams of information.

The first and simplest element is managers' or entrepreneurs' experience. Leaders building strategic hypotheses should have knowledge and experience, otherwise their intuitions will be either trivial or most probably wrong.

R. Mohn, who made Bertelsmann one of the biggest media corporations in the world, started from developing the sale of books and extremely successful 'Book of the Month' clubs all over the world (in a sign of the times division was restructured and finally closed in 2011), taking advantage of long years of tradition and his personal experience in running a family publishing house. Yet in another example it was probably R. Kroc's marketing and sale experience that permitted him to see potential in a bar run by the McDonald brothers selling hamburgers – a potential not seen by the owners themselves. Similarly H. Schulz imagined the potential of a Starbucks cafe, founded first in the rainy Seattle. D. Mateschitz, in turn, noticed the global potential in an Asiatic energy drink Red Bull – greater than its founders actually did. Many Polish entrepreneurs who were successful in the 1990s had already had previous business experience, for example J. Starak transmitted his experience from the first company named Comindex, established in the 1980s, into other companies in pharmaceutical and food sectors later on; T. Chmiel started to build his furniture empire Black Red White at the beginning of the 1980s; and I. Eris and H. Orfinger developed one of the most valuable brands in Poland and found the very successful cosmetic company Dr Irena Eris Cosmetic Laboratory few years later.

Both entrepreneurs and company leaders have an ability to link elements of reality into a single new picture and complement their experience or imagination in ways different from other market players. And they don't do it in a simple way. Experience allows them to work out sophisticated analysis schemes, which like a filter reject some fragments of reality, seeking for other patterns, atypical dependences and new opportunities.

When do we know that strategists' experience will really count? All research shows that three conditions are the most important: prolonged practice, a 'kind' learning environment and an opportunity to create expert schemas or worldviews.[11] Some people might be fast learners, but a real experience and expertise takes long time to develop. There is a growing consensus that roughly 10,000 hours of deliberate practice is needed to acquire high professional expertise and collection of skills in particular domain.[12] It means years of practice that should take place in an environment that fosters learning. This second condition is crucially important, because an environment that allows to develop and hone real professional skills should be relatively regular and predictable. Nobel laureate Daniel Kahnemann discuss this issue in details, stressing that only regular environments that provide quick and relevant feedback with clear and real consequences for failure allow to develop skilled intuitions and experience: 'Chess is an extreme example of a regular environment, but bridge and poker also provide robust statistical regularities that can support skill. Physicians, nurses, athletes, and firefighters also face complex but fundamentally orderly situations... In contrast, stock pickers and political scientists who make long-term forecasts operate in a zero-validity environment. Their failures reflects the basic unpredictability of the events that they try to forecast.'[13] Hence a good business environment that helps to develop useful experience can be complex but it cannot be very volatile, because in very dynamic environments it is almost impossible to learn regularities and create expert schemas, patterns or worldviews that help to make sense of environmental changes and develop a good strategy.

All three conditions are related. A Belgian family business Palm Breweries had had many years of experience in producing flavor and wheat beer that enabled it to conquer the Belgian market, and they definitely were able to develop expert schemas and patterns of action. It transmitted the experience in 1999 into Poland, investing in the construction of a modern brewery and copied its Belgian business model. Unfortunately it turned out that Polish business environment is much more volatile than Belgian and after years of attempting to change reality, the Belgians gave up and sold the brewery to SABMiller in 2007.

The second crucial element is the ability to holistically analyze reality and to notice links between almost obvious things – faster than others. There is a well-known anecdote that illustrates this ability well. Two economists walk down the street and suddenly one of them notices a 100-dollar bill on the pavement and says: 'Look, there's a 100-dollar bill.' The other economist replies: 'That's impossible, if there had been a 100 dollars, someone would have already taken it!' Market opportunities are like the banknotes on the ground. Most people are not able to notice the banknote or believe it is out there. And this is exactly the ability which distinguishes entrepreneurs. This is why we say that they are able to create and notice market opportunities where other people see just normality.

What do entrepreneurs and strategists see? Research shows that they see more and in a different way and that it is something people can learn because these are skills that are a function of experience and process of constant learning.[14] They allow strategists like experienced chess players, race drivers or surgeons, to make holistic and fast judgments through identifying relationships between the elements and not the elements themselves. When there are significant technological changes (e.g. Internet, mobile phones), demographic changes (life expectancy raises by roughly 2.5 years every 10 years in developed countries!), social changes (late marriage and a smaller number of children, educational boom), organizational changes (outsourcing and offshoring), they are basically seen by everyone, which doesn't mean that many managers can look at them in a systematic way, recognize certain patterns and structures and treat them as a strategic building blocks.[15] Strategists learn this unique ability to see reality holistically, grasp the meaning of relationships and connect the dots, by experience accumulated in particular domain: 'Because complex schemas develop in a particular domain (one's area of expertise), they are more likely to lead to effective decisions in that domain than when used in a different domain or context. Thus, complex managerial schemas may serve a manager well at the office but may lead to inaccurate intuitive judgments at home.'[16]

An example of such holistic judgment can be a set of decisions by L. Quingde and his associates to change radically the profile of the company Galanz. Founded at the beginning of the Chinese transformation in 1978, as Guizhou Down Products Factory, it was one of thousands of textile factories constructed in the South of China, in the Guandong province. At the end of the 1980s, the market for textiles and clothes became extremely competitive in China and low-entry barriers resulted in a further growth of competitors' number. Companies from the sector made standard moves. A small, financially strong group followed the way of building their own brands, other players became their suppliers and finally a large percentage of companies copied Western brands. Some companies decided to integrate backwards (e.g. Man Tin, which became a huge jeans producer), others opted for a forward integration building distribution networks. In the meantime, at the turn of the 1980s and 1990s, L. Quingde and other managers made a careful industry analysis and came to the conclusion that there was simply no future in it. After a year of debates and assessments of market trends and opportunities the leaders decided to move the company toward the household appliance market! Galanz bought technology and equipment from Toshiba (after long negotiations, because Galanz was not an established partner) and in 1992 it started a new life as a producer of microwaves. The choice of this segment was the result of two observations. On one hand, it was a fast-growing segment of kitchen equipment in China, and on the other hand margins of most world producers had come close to zero so they started to look for cheap suppliers. Galanz noticed its chance as a subcontractor (as an *OEM – Original Equipment Manufacturer*) for brand producers thanks to very low production costs in China. In 1996 Galanz produced for over 250 international corporations, but did so in a distinctive way. Within letters of agreements it required partners to hand over their factories, transferred them to China and with some technological support it produced as an OEM, thereby acquiring access to technology and constantly raising its output. Its factories operate in a three-shift system (140 hours per week approximately year round), employees earn between 100 and 145 dollars per month that allows the company to take good advantage from assets and low labor costs. In 1993 it produced 10,000 items and in 2006 over 22 million, becoming the biggest world producer of microwaves.[17]

In a similar vein post-communist countries were a laboratory of such local opportunities in the 1990s. A huge economic boom and the appearance of new markets and products created both great opportunities and problems for consumers. A typical example is the tile market. Consumers in this region in the 1980s could only choose from one type of tile and two or three different colors – which facilitated the decision. In the 1990s there was a market explosion. But after taking advantage of the first opportunities, hundreds of suppliers appeared, as well as thousands of colors, sizes and types of tiles. They created a totally new consumer problem – an excess of possibilities and a difficulty with choosing among the myriad of choices. Where everyone saw thousands of possible choices and frustrated customers, managers of Kolo Sanitec (leading bathroom ceramics specialist) noticed a new opportunity in linking those elements into a pattern. Together with interior designers, they built an interesting holistic solution for toilets and bathrooms and allowed customers to buy ready solutions (a total bathroom, for example) instead of worrying about matching the tiles. This move allowed those companies to develop an interesting strategy and a competitive advantage, but also a new market segment, which after a while obviously became the target of other entrepreneurs.

Finally there are many such opportunities at the micro level – concrete products, services, behaviors and new technologies. In retrospect, they often seem obvious and trivial: comfortable and fashionable carriers for babies, which are simply a different version of baby wrappers, in which women had wrapped their babies for thousands years; green food; a nice grocery shop like British Waiterose; a mobile hairdresser, who delivers his or her services at the customer's home; LCD panels hung displaying advertisement in office building elevators or a special swinging armchair (the so-called glider rocking chair, which moves horizontally) as a chair for women feeding their babies. Their obviousness can only be seen when someone builds a company around them. The task of a strategist is to holistically see the environment and to build around this view a thorough analysis of data as well as the ability to translate trends, changes and fragments of reality into precise local opportunities. It has to be done relatively fast in order to use them as material to build a company strategy before other managers do the same.

Since the world is not simple, even trends and opportunities can change under the influence of the market situation. When SABMiller bought the aforementioned Belgian brewery in Poland, it had a huge experience as the leader of the Polish market and its perception of reality was rather unequivocal. The company didn't have spare production capacity to meet demand, the market was growing by over 10 percent annually and the Belgians were ready to sell quite a modern brewery. It could seem that it was difficult to find a better combination and the hypothesis that an acquisition and development of the brewery was a good strategic move was logical. But in the meantime the crisis of 2008 came and the market collapsed. The company faced a totally different situation – a decreasing demand and an excessive production capacity. This resulted in a radical strategy change, a liquidation of investments and the closing of the brewery.

The third element of building strategic hypotheses is imagination, worthy almost of Hamlet's famous phrase: '*me thinks I see. Where (…) In my mind's eye, Horatio.*' A genuine strategist doesn't see a phantom (although even that can happen in rare and temporary moments of pessimism), but he or she tries to put together pieces of information, facts, supposition and speculation into a new picture of reality, to imagine a new reality or even different new realities which can be formed based on the launch of a given strategy. Imagination allows experimentation with creative options and creates the possibility space of new futures.[18] I recall that in a group that a famous Polish entrepreneur Mariusz Łukasiewicz brought together to develop the strategy for a new bank (named later Eurobank) in Poland. We had a classic conflict between analysis and imagination. A sober and methodical data analysis told us nobody needed a new bank. Quite the contrary – there were too many banks on the Polish and European market. But the experience and imagination of Łukasiewicz told him there were still many variants of entry strategies and a lot of space for new business models. He convinced all of us to work on new options and finally three different full-blooded visions were born.

The first one was a mobile bank for relatively wealthy customers, a sort of 'Ducatti' model for the High Net Worth Individuals. The second was a traditional 'brick-and-mortar' boutique bank for well-off young, urban professionals. The most interesting option within this model was a bank for women only. A third business model was a simple bank specializing in a fast service based on subsidiaries and stands in hypermarkets and commercial centers ('McDonald's' model). Each of these visions was a potential strategy as was built with a different, incomplete and uncertain picture of future reality. We finally followed the third option and Eurobank became a huge success story, as a simple consumer-loans oriented bank.

An Egyptian entrepreneur Onsi Sawiris created over the period of 20 years a powerful, multibillion-dollar company Orascom Group, mainly in the business of mobile telecommunications, construction, hotels and media. He started in his motherland but developed and grew also in the most difficult markets of Africa and Asia. The imagination and passion of Sawiris allowed him to bravely enter markets in the developing world, which frightened Western operators because they were poor, unstable or involved in wars. The Orascom Group now operates for example in such difficult markets as Pakistan, Algeria, Congo, Togo, Chad Bangladesh or North Korea.

Another distinguished entrepreneur, Subhash Chandra, created an Indian business empire Essen Group, operating in fields such as media, construction, adventure parks, basic education, packaging, lotteries and micro finance. Each new business initiative is a result of his outstanding imagination which has allowed him to notice opportunities faster

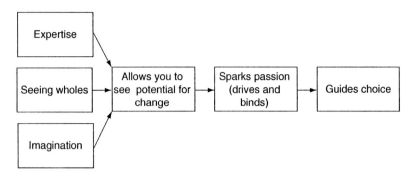

Figure 2.1   Passion as a driver of strategy

than others and to found first companies in any given industry market. Chandra speaks about perceiving opportunities in the following way: 'It is my belief that this depends on the talents one has. This talent is different from skills, knowledge or experience. These three things can be acquired, transferred or taught, but talent is by birth. Being able to smell opportunity before others is because of talent.'[19] Since his latest initiative is an American television channel Veria, a channel devoted to natural lifestyle, linked to a web site and a network of spas, it is possible that the risky hypothesis of Chandra that the society of the US grows to a healthy lifestyle will turn out to be right. However, strategy as a hypothesis is only an approximation and a simplification, which needs to be translated into a set of final choices and then precise initiatives, exactly like Sawiris has accomplished this by widening the activity of Orascom Group, like Chandra has done by building Essen Group or like Łukasiewicz has done by creating Eurobank.

The way all three elements connect is shown in Figure 2.1. Expertise, holistic perspective and imagination combined allow one to see potential for innovation or development, generally – for change. These spark passion and guide strategic choices aimed at exploration and exploitation of change potential.

So what? Passion and decisions

The essence of each strategy are key choices – decisions regarding what the organization wants to achieve and how it wants to do it. It seems trivial but it is not. Entrepreneurial companies actually go through three states of aggregation – from gas, through liquid to solid.[20] In its point of departure every company is just a gas – a legal shell in form of a company with a certain minimum initial capital. With time, quickly or slowly, the company transforms into a liquid state, it is poured with money (in form of revenue and retained profit), property, machinery and equipment infrastructure (called assets), people (frustrated or satisfied, but always not accepting the fact that they are a source generating growing fixed costs in form of a payroll fund) and nonmaterial resources (brands, patents and knowledge).

Many companies remain in a liquid state for a long time and can do many things – the more they do, the more universal their assets and the less specialized their employees are. Of course the type of equipment and employees imposes limitations – lines to fill bottles will not be useful to bake bread or stuff sausages. Limitations always exist – even a company that is just a legal entity has in its statutes a definite set of approved types of activity it can perform, and usually it cannot venture into healthcare, foreign affairs or weapons trading. The liquid state imposes additional boundaries but still allows great flexibility. The company can sell a given type of equipment, purchase new machinery and quite freely move from one activity to another. Turbulent years of the 1990s in times of the Central Europe transformation saw hundreds of thousands of such 'liquid' companies. Entrepreneurs moved in such a way from the production of fruit juices to the field of finance, from the production of motorcycle fairings to industrial automatics, or from selling bananas to production of sweets and later to service and production of equipment for telecommunications and finally moving to the real estate market.

A company moves into a solid state when we introduce an additional but a very abstract element – the basic strategic idea. This idea can exist already in the moment of the firm's founding, being a derivation of the founders' dreams and passion, but these are relatively rare cases in practice. In most cases such an idea matures slowly. Masaru Ibuka didn't have any key strategy idea when he created Sony in 1946, starting from ideas to produce soups with sugar, clubs for miniature golf, rulers and pots to boil rice. The founder of the biggest chain of supermarkets in the world, Wal-Mart, Sam Walton, started in the 1950s from a franchise of a Franklin's shop selling virtually everything and anything in a small town of Newport in Arkansas, USA. When Terry Gou founded Hon Hai Precision Industry Company in 1974, he created one of many Taiwanese firms producing mechanical and electric components. But thanks to the strategy of total vertical integration, 30 years later the company, widely known by its trade name Foxconn, became the world's biggest producer of both components and electronic products. Factories of the same company often produce competing products, for example, consoles such as Playstation, Wii and Xbox 360. The idea of the strategy by Sony, Wal-Mart, Foxconn and many other successful initiatives matured slowly, with the companies maturing to take decisions to concentrate on determined products and markets, shape a business model and build a competitive advantage.

Time is needed because no solid company strategy can be born without an appropriate mixture of passion, intuition, thorough analysis of data and, most importantly, time. The variety of firms and situations results in cases of short-term successes of unfinished strategies, either as a result of a coincidence or a heroic involvement of company members. But basing success only on fortunate coincidences is not only risky but also unnecessary. A genuine strategist has a better recipe for success – a combination of passion, intuition and reliable analysis. It is important that as a consequence of a maturing basic strategic idea the number of strategic choices decreases. These are choices that stabilize the organization's activity because they dictate the decision on what and how the company wants to do and what it should not do. In this sense these are choices that give it its identity but decrease the general flexibility by creating binding limitations to organizational decisions. Thanks to key choices the firm becomes more unequivocal and unique – it starts to have a strategy.

The basic idea, changing the firm's state from liquid to solid, decreases the organization's flexibility. It is an old paradox of strategy and a problem with which academics and practitioners constantly cope – is it possible to create a flexible strategy, or is this term an oxymoron because strategy and flexibility are mutually exclusive? In typical examples unequivocal strategic choices limit flexibility because they define what the firm does and how it does it and what it cannot or shall not do. In practice this means making choices with regard to a concrete market, product and service specification (with a low or high quality, low or high price), ways of distribution (via Internet, direct deliveries and sale through modern distribution channels) as well as ways of production. Since the launch takes place in conditions of uncertain reality, ordinary care would dictate a minimum flexibility during the launch in order to allow for a margin for reaction to unexpected events and anomalies. While it is a directionally correct recommendation, it must be clearly stated that in practice it is costly (and this means a decrease in strategy's effectiveness) and technically difficult.

It is well illustrated by the history of Cray Computer Corporation – a producer of the fastest computers in the world (the so-called supercomputers) for scientific, military and industrial calculations. In the 1980s it was one of the favorite academic examples of a good differentiation strategy. The example was very distinct as a niche differentiation strategy and the computers themselves were technologically outstanding, esthetically beautiful and unusually expensive. Unfortunately, the company faced major problems shortly after it became a famous example of a good differentiation and focused strategy, for which it is difficult to blame both the company and the theory of strategy. Computers continued to be excellent but two things occurred which the company couldn't cope with. The communist system with the Warsaw Pact collapsed and suddenly the demand of the main customer – that is, the American army and governmental agencies – disappeared and substitute technologies appeared – technologies of parallel data processing, which were cheaper and simpler than technologies used by supercomputers. Cray went bankrupt because it was unable to adapt to changes, which hit the basis of its functioning – the market and the technologies. Of course it could have (and for a certain time it even tried) worked on technologies of parallel data processing but this meant lack of concentration, political battles for allocation of resources for research and development, increased fluctuation of the best personnel and internal competition. Cray constitutes a good warning, an example of a firm that made its strategic choices in such a specific way that its strategy became unequivocal but totally inflexible. Such situations should be avoided since 'final choices' should always allow for a margin for fitting and adaptation, remembering that the price of increasing adaptability will be slightly higher costs of operations.

Through key choices the company commits to a certain way of acting, which is long lasting and costly, so practically irreversible in the short and medium run. There is, however, a question, which choices are really strategic in the mass of decisions taken by managers. Organizations constantly change after all. They grow or become smaller, they purchase other companies or get rid of parts of their operations. They change their structures, processes and technologies. One way to distinguish strategic choices is intention – whether they were treated as such in the very moment of taking the decision. A better way, in my opinion, is the analysis of consequences which joins both intentions and effects. Genuinely key strategic choices have two natural and mutually strengthening consequences – inertia (lock-in) and exclusion (lock-out).[21]

Inertia and exclusion

Strategic choices are distinct in that they give companies an unavoidable inertia – companies stick to their once-made choices for a long time. On the intellectual level strategy can be changed relatively quickly – it is enough to conduct an analysis of environment and simply work out a new concept for action. In practice, however, every fundamental strategic change is a huge emotional, time-consuming and capital-consuming cost. It is not easy at all to get rid of dedicated assets (such as a chemical installation, a film production studio, a printing press, a network of retail shops or to change the organizational culture), and such action brings risks which are difficult to assess. This is why sometimes organizations get locked in a particular strategy by initial choices and prefer to die rather than change their strategic choices and way of acting.[22] This phenomenon has been elegantly named by D. Miller as the 'Icarus paradox', showing empirical trajectories of strategic decisions' inertia leading companies to a collapse.[23]

Strategic choices also mean exclusion and opportunity costs – they simply mean a lock-out or resignation from a certain set of opportunities and from another possible way of acting (as it was the case of Cray Computer Corporation), which would have required other market choices and organizational resources. Time plays a role – even if the firm could still consider using old opportunities and change or widen its profile, most frequently those opportunities have been used and the place on the market has been taken. As Heraclitus put it – 'no man ever steps into the same river twice'. This is why the higher the costs of acquiring new resources, forming new skills and reactivating old opportunities, the bigger the firm's keenness to stick with their choices in a kind of inertia. Strategic choices make a sort of a funnel – once you get in, it is very difficult to get out. Whether we like it or not, many managers, trying to avoid such a situation, avoid making difficult choices and de facto firms don't have any strategy. Let's have a look at the example of IKEA, which illustrates key choices well and permits a better understanding of the logic of inertia and exclusion (Figure 2.2). The main strategic choices of IKEA have been unchanged for many years, unequivocal and strictly linked to each other.[24]

The company produces good, modular, but quite ephemeral furniture (and it stresses their temporary character in its advertisements!). It minimizes the cost of design and production by placing manufacturing plants in countries with low costs, including China and Poland, among others, and reaching a large scale of production. The scale is

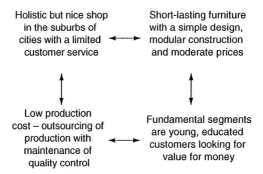

Figure 2.2   Strategic choices of IKEA

additionally increased by the systematic process of internationalization. The location of shops (in the suburbs of towns, where the cost of land acquisition is lower), their size and layout as well as the way products are displayed makes an impression of a friendly shop, on one hand, and reduces the need for customer service on the other. Sales volume and fast rotation allows IKEA to offer a very wide range of products at relatively low prices, and low costs ensure IKEA excellent margins. This is why IKEA copies its strategy and business model throughout the whole world in a practically unchanged way, and every employee and customer can understand them looking at one simple figure. The inertia of IKEA's strategy is de facto enormous and sometimes it brings trouble. For example, during the expansion in the American market it turned out that the size of its beds, cupboards, tables and even glasses (American pizza and ice cubes are bigger than Europeans!) is not adjusted to customer expectations.[25] After initially denying the problem, IKEA finally adjusted its products and the way it designs and builds furniture have become advantageous in the process of adapting products to local conditions. At the same time these choices allowed IKEA to build the brand, key competencies and resources in a very specific area of products and markets; their migration to other markets (production of cars or electronics) would have been very difficult, costly and time-consuming. IKEA has been and will always be within the foreseeable future the producer of furniture and household equipment and its ability to adapt is limited to the launch of a restaurant, additional shops and a playground for children. There is nothing wrong with this because IKEA is very consistent and passionate in its key choices and logic of its strategy, taking care of the disciplined realization of those choices in practice.

Discipline is an indispensable element of the process of building strategy because even the greatest passion may not endure the clash with reality and competition. The simplest reason is a situation where a company doesn't have enough resources to implement the strategy in practice – this is the fate of many entrepreneurs. Ryanair entered aggressively and effectively the Irish and British market of passenger air transport in May 1986 as a result of the wave of deregulation. It entered the market with the strategy of low prices and good service. It went in the financial spin less than five years later, in January 1991. It had a lot of passion but too little discipline in its implementation of strategy. Every strategy implementation demands solutions for which neither the theory, nor the practice, have simple, unequivocal answers. We need to approach them in a complex way considering the four interrelated processes which constitute the essence of the discipline of strategy.

3
Discipline of Strategy Execution: Sensemaking and Territory

Who is the decision-maker?

A very rich literature in the field of leadership focuses mainly on styles and methods of effective operations. Researchers have come a long way – from theories linking effective leadership with personality character- istics and charisma, through situational and evolutionary leadership theories and concepts of transformation leadership, to have recently returned to the conclusion that personality features indeed play an important role after all. The latest statement was born thanks to the con- cept of emotional intelligence.[1] It is very difficult to define the essence of leadership and the features of good leaders, but it is possible to clearly define their role and the tasks, for which they are responsible. Regardless of personality or leadership style, company leaders constitute an indis- pensable and fundamental link in four interactive processes showed in Figure 3.1:

1) interpretation and sensemaking of environmental context,
2) defining goals and priorities,
3) defining company boundaries,
4) building a business model.

It is a specific know-how of strategy execution, which must be imple- mented in an intellectually and organizationally disciplined way. Not all leaders will equally effectively manage each of these processes. However, they have to be effective enough in order to make sure that each of them is conducted fairly effectively and constitutes an intellectual contribu- tion for the remaining processes. Possible mistakes and incoherencies have to be detected and corrected sufficiently fast.

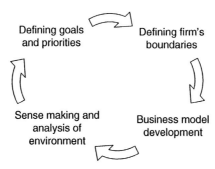

Figure 3.1   Discipline of strategy execution

Obviously, when looking for information and capabilities indispensable to carrying out these activities and taking decisions, leaders can and should make use of the knowledge of the remaining members of the organization as well as consultants and academics representing various scientific fields. They also can and should delegate the implementation of large fragments of these processes. One of the best supervisory boards, in which I have participated, used to invite to its sessions anthropologists, sociologists, specialists in communication technologies and experienced managers. In such a company we discussed, for example, market predictions and hypotheses regarding the future social and cultural trends in the company environment.

Many companies regularly organize meetings of top and middle managers. Some of them have a ceremonial character, but in most companies they are devoted to discussions on the present and future company situation. One cannot think about and discuss the strategy of a tech company without understanding the trajectory of technological changes, which is usually (not always – as innovator's dilemma shows!) best known by employees of research and development departments.[2] One cannot create a vision for a fashion company without discussions with designers, sellers and customers. Gathering and processing information, as well as discussions, can and even should take place among a large group of top and middle managers, specialists and other stakeholders, because it can contribute to two goals.

First, it allows leaders to have access to additional information and opinions and to broaden the extent of the considered alternatives of action. It is an enlargement of the base of resources and experience. It is also an amplification of the holistic overview of the reality as well as of imagination, needed to appropriately formulate the strategy in the form of a hypothesis as well as to make appropriate choices. Second, it builds an emotional commitment of company members, especially middle managers, to the implementation of the chosen strategy. It can be called employee engagement, co-optation, benefiting from employee potential and experience, creation of commitment or emotional intelligence. No matter the wording, it is necessary and advantageous for each party. No wonder that it is commonly thought that a democratic contribution of many company members to the construction of the company strategy, together with taking decisions, constitutes a need and a requirement of today.[3] I only partially agree with that. Discussing and decision-making are two different things. Whereas a variety of competent voices enriches and refreshes the discussion, the quality of company decisions is usually reversely proportional to the number of persons who took them. Final decisions within each of these four key processes should be taken by a small group of managers from the highest level of the company hierarchy – the company leaders. They should be the ones accountable for them. They are the only ones to make decisive sense of phenomena in the company environment, and based on that to make strategic choices, to set company boundaries, goals and priorities and to approve a business model of company operations. They are also the only ones to communicate these decisions to the environment and to employees in a reliable way and to defend effectively the strategy's simplicity and coherence. Therefore, in the best meaning of this word, they are the guardians of discipline of the main strategic processes.

The processes of debate and decision-making should have an interactive character. They should constitute a periodically repetitive exercise, in which leaders and managers are obliged to requestion the approved arrangements, analyze them in a critical way and check whether the approved company responses still make sense as well as to ensure the strategy's simplicity and coherence. The question arises whether it matters which of these questions we ask first. The most logical and reasonable is the following sequence: *make sense of outside world – set goals – define company boundaries – develop a business model*. In practice, the logic of this sequence is often subject to changes and situational adjustments. First, when the point of departure of a strategy is – as it should be – a true passion, a dream to change or create a market, it will most often dictate mutually interrelated choices. Therefore, the sequence stops existing and one needs to work on all four processes simultaneously, because the way we see the world will influence the definition of company boundaries and this in turn will influence possible goals and the development of a business model. Second, when we create a strategy, in most cases we do not start from zero. Either we have an existing company with an already-made set of choices, or we use certain market patterns or examples of good or bad strategies and competitive behaviors. So the company already has certain business logic, goals, market and product domain as well as an initial business model. When leaders decide to choose a new intellectual (even broad) concept of strategy, they decide when to start the process of change. Modification of any of these elements makes other elements adapt, because strategy requires adaptation of all choices and activities. In one company, a pragmatic point of departure can be reconstruction of the business model, in another change of boundaries, in yet another choice of long-term goals, which every textbook recommends. There are many possible ways but it is important to know what the target destination is.

Sensemaking of an environmental dynamics – a rule of hinge

There are possibly still industries and companies which operate in a relatively stable environment, but it is ever more difficult to find them. Deregulation, globalization, blurring of industries' boundaries and technological progress make the environment of most companies so complex, dynamic or even chaotic that it is difficult to understand the logics of changes taking place in it. However, a rescue for managers can be the fact that the world is not entirely predictable, but does not work in a random way as well.

First, many changes in the company environment take place slowly, have an incremental character and certain logics of development. Some changes, for example, demographic changes, can be described with a good function of the trend and analyzed in terms of the trend's consequences. Others, for example, technological or economic changes, most often have the shape of an 'S' curve. They start with weak signals, which later strengthen and finally a radical change takes place. The impact of the radical change weakens with the time the companies need to adapt to it. The problem is obviously that even knowing the general function of the trend, it is difficult to predict when the accumulation of small, progressive changes will create a new quality and on what it will actually depend. Therefore, unexpected events and breakthroughs are unavoidable, because they are actually hidden in each statistical variance, and they have to occur every now and then, still constituting a surprise.

Fortunately, such occurrences are relatively rare. They are wild cards – like black swans.

Second, most changes are generated by the very same actors of the environment – customers, competitors, regulative bodies. Their actions are visible and to some degree inertial, and therefore the company can follow them on a daily basis as well as assess their importance and impact from the point of view of its own actions.

Third, the business environment has its history and many contemporary changes have their past analogies, which it is worth going back to. Today's uncertainty in the environment of the world of media, provoked by the radical development of the Internet, has its analogy in the media revolution, which was created by mass television in the 1950s. The 2008 bubble of the stock exchange market, in turn, resembled the bubble created by unrealistic estimations of the value of Internet companies at the end of the 1990s. Perhaps we wouldn't have experienced a global financial crisis in 2008 if managers and administrations had better known the economic history.

Fourth, even in a very complex and dynamic reality, there are some general rules. Looking back with today's perspective at the years toward the end of the 1990s, the boom of dotcoms and the wild predictions of the birth of New Economy, one has to wonder why so many people forgot the simplest rules of business operations. P. Saffo is right in noticing that in the economic environment 'plenty new was happening, but underlying the revolution were deep, unchanging consumer desires, and ultimately, to the sorrow of many a start-up, unchanging laws of economics. By focusing on the novelties, many missed the fact that consumers were using their new broadband links to buy very traditional items like books and engage in old human activities like gossip, entertainment and pornography. And though the future-lookers pronounced it to be a time when the old rules no longer applied, the old economic imperatives applied with a vengeance and the dot-com bubble burst just like every other bubble before it. Anyone who had taken the time to examine the history of economic bubbles would have seen it coming'.[4]

The incremental character of most changes, historical conditions, stability of actors acting in the environment and some rules of the game make it easier to carry out the first task of company leaders when developing a strategy – making sense of phenomena in the complex and dynamic business environment. They should look at the complex world around the company and patiently search for a hidden order in it – much the same way a good chess player, looking at any given moment of time on the layout of figures and pawns on the chessboard, is looking for a pattern that will allow him or her to create a further winning game concept. In order to do this, they have to first answer several critical questions. These answers should make it possible to develop a coherent and effective concept of acting. Each textbook in the field of strategic management presents many tools for such an analysis – from the analysis of threats and opportunities in the close and distant environment, through the PEST analysis (political and legal, economic, social and technological conditions and trends), the development of scenarios, the analysis of Porter's 5 forces, strategic groups, the stakeholders' analysis, the marketing segmentation and so on. The problem with these analyses is that as a result of them, we usually obtain a long report, in which it is difficult to find a true sense and focus. In other words it is difficult to find in it one, two or three really important phenomena, on which the entire company attention and strategy should concentrate.

I suggest it be called a 'hinge rule'. A thorough analysis of the environment should allow leaders of the company to find among many phenomena taking place in the environment a 'hinge', on which they can hang the company strategy. Theorists of strategy represent two dominant and competing views on the role of changes and trends in the company environment when developing a strategy.[5] The first view claims that managers, using their predictive tools, and especially analyses of trends and scenarios, are able to predict with a high probability the main course of environmental changes. The characteristics of changes discussed above favor this view – their incremental and cumulative character, historical repetitiveness, common sources (customers, competitors and regulative bodies) and existence of general economic rules. Additionally, at any given moment of time and in each industry, there are some typical key success factors, which have ensured success to most companies. They often become a basis to develop effective strategies by large or small firms. A good example is the search for economy of scale as a key strategy of virtually all of today's steel producers, like ArcelorMittal, Baosteel Group, Pohang Iron and Steel, Tata Steel, Nucor Steel, Severstal or Ezz Steel. Recreating the pattern of changes and extrapolating it for the future, leaders can define with a high probability the resources and investments necessary to develop a sustainable competitive advantage on the market. This view assumes that strategy can and should be developed in a formal, ordered way according to the sequence: environmental analysis (trends, scenarios and key success factors) – organization's diagnosis (strengths and weaknesses) – choice of the strategy linking future states of the environment, strengths and weaknesses of the organization and the undertaken business initiatives.

The second view assumes that knowledge about the environment is of little use in the practice of strategic management. The main argument is that nearly every organization can benefit from a thorough analysis in a similar way. Therefore strategies elaborated and based on this knowledge will be similar, and that is why organizations cannot develop a real competitive advantage through these strategies. Hence, the proponents of this view argue that the key focus of strategists should be on relatively rare, violent and little probable abnormalities in the environmental phenomena. These are classical moments of the Schumpeterian creative destruction, an occurrence of radical opportunities or dramatic threats. Examples of such occurrences can be new technologies (e.g. mobile phone), a political change (collapse of communism, the emergence of China as one of the superpowers), an economic change (great crisis of 2008 that shook many industries – from finance to tourism), a social change (greying of the Western societies, multiculturalism of national states). As consequences of such developments are difficult to predict, the essence of strategy is an active entrepreneurial orientation. Strategy should be under such circumstances a plan for how to gain access to resources (not necessarily to possess them) and a plan to acquire the ability of using special skills.

Both these views are theoretically coherent, but from a purely logical perspective, they are of a limited practical value. The assumption that managers can fairly precisely predict the future – and develop a better strategy – is very improbable. It is also contrary to the results of most empirical research, which shows that managers, trying to work out a map of a complex environment submitted to systematic breakthroughs, usually behave economically – which does not mean that the result of such behavior is fully rational.[6] Actually, while conducting an analysis of the environment, managers are most often driven by three factors – the degree to which it is subject to change, the degree of its complexity and the degree to which it is relevant at a given moment in time. If the perceived relevance and dynamism have a motivating impact on the overview and analysis of the environment, the perceived complexity strongly limits the organization's activities related to gathering information. The more complex the environment becomes, the more often managers decrease the intensiveness of their analysis and tend to concentrate their attention on a relatively small number of important issues and stakeholders. Such a simplified view of the world makes it difficult to work out a good map of the environment and does not make it easier to act effectively.

The second view, that the essence of strategy is an active waiting for opportunities is interesting, but risky.[7] We simply cannot predict when these revolutionary opportunities will appear, nor can we know how to prepare for them. Therefore, it seems that the proposed 'rule of hinge' links the best sides of both these views. Of course, it would be best to discover revolutionary opportunities before others, but their unpredictable nature does not allow for it. At the same time, environment has its logic of change, which can and should be understood. That is why the product of the analysis of the environment should not describe all important and possible phenomena and processes, but make sense of the complex and dynamic reality. And making sense signifies extracting from this complex picture one or two circumstances or trends, which to our view constitute the key raw material to develop a strategy, a hook, on which we can hang our choices. Of course, there is an element of speculation included here, but a thorough analysis can make this speculation more reliable.

For the emerging Polish giant company Atlas (a producer of chemical construction materials under Atlas and Aval brands), whose strategy will be discussed in more detail later, the hinge was the observation of a gap between immense demand for tiles and construction materials in the 1990s, dispersion of distribution networks and lack of good technologies to glue ceramic tiles to the bathroom walls. The strategy of Atlas – to integrate the product with the process of training workers to use it – turned out to be unusually effective, enabled them to corner much more powerful MNCs in this industry and made them the leading producer in Poland and one of the largest in Europe. In the development of Tele-Fonika Kable, the biggest producer of copper and aluminum cables and wires in Central Europe, as well as in the development of Elsewedy Cables – the Egyptian giant in this field, the role of hinge was substantiated by the constantly increasing demand for electric energy and telecommunication wires in the whole region. Both companies followed the increasing demand, effectively making the most classical strategic moves – developing production capacities, overtaking competitors, broadening offer, improving service quality, keeping a flexible price policy and systematically internationalizing their operations. The hinge of the pace of the market's development constitutes the point of departure of many Asian companies. In the Deloitte ranking of the fastest-growing technological Asian companies in 2011, the two first places were taken by

The Store Corporation (China) and Silicon Mitus Inc (South Korea).The former grew by 19,218 percent (!) between 2007 and 2010, developing a one-stop shopping platform for everyday items. Silicon Mitus grew more slowly, 'only' by 9336 percent, exploiting the unprecedented dynamics of growth on the market for semiconductors, components and electronics around the world. In the same ranking in 2012, the first two places were taken by ProCrystal Technology (Taiwan) and Vipshop Holding (China). The former grew between by 10,027 percent between 2008 and 2011, in relatively mature sector of semiconductors, components and electronics. The latter is the leading online discount retailer for brands in China, and it grew in a similar period by 7988 percent.[8]

The hinge of Apple's strategy on the market of mobile phones was in turn the observation of two facts: high cost of phone subsidies by telecommunication operators combined with an increasing dependence on the Internet of all users of mobile phones. Everyone was aware of it, but not many drew the same conclusions. This is why the initial concept of an iPhone as a smartphone, a multifunction communication device ('Internet in a pocket', as Steve Jobs put it), for which the user had to pay a full price (400–500 dollars) was so attractive for the biggest American operator AT&T that it even agreed to share a part of income from phone fares.

In the example of Brazilian company Embraer, further discussed in the next section, the hinge was noticing that the fast growth of discount airlines would create a great demand for small (50-seater) aircrafts with a regional range. Another hinge was a hypothetical but reliable assumption that the increasing competition of low-cost and normal airlines, and the cost reduction stemming from it, would create a demand for bigger (100-seater) aircrafts with a regional range.

In order not to present one-sided examples, it must be highlighted that sometimes the chosen 'hinge' can turn out to be reasonable almost by coincidence. This is illustrated by M. Raynor in his fascinating analysis of the well-known fight between standards such as VHS (Matsushita) and Betamax (Sony).[9] Both companies introduced their innovative standards after an attempt to conquer the market with a tape player by CTI, which hadn't been successful. The technology turned out to be too complicated, unhandy (a standard recording took 114 minutes) and had weak distribution channels. Under conditions of high uncertainty with regard to customer and film suppliers' preferences, Sony and Matsushita decided to opt for different standards and separate strategies based on their key competences. Briefly, Sony assumed that a tape player would be used mainly to record existing programs from television and the key feature for customers would be the convenience and quality of performance as well as the chance to avoid watching advertisements. Using its competencies, Sony designed a modern, refined Betamax player, which had both playback and fast forward functions. Matsushita assumed that the most important feature for the customer would be the price (which derives from Matsushita's competence – a low cost of production) and the basic function of the player would be watching films at home. Both visions of the future reality were equally probable, and initially the Betamax standard was winning. However, nobody predicted the speed of the growth of the rental business, which by the way, was against film producers' interests, fearing illegal recording – much the same way music producers fight peer-to-peer exchange today. Therefore, film producers supported videodisc as a desirable technology. Today, who even remembers the technology by Philips, which was, at the time, a real competitor with tapes, and in the opinion of many people and companies was expected to become the standard in the future!

In the meantime, the market for rentals started a life of its own and doubled between 1982 and 1986. Rental shops, most often the property of entrepreneurs with a limited capital, preferred the VHS standard, because it was cheaper and allowed for recording a longer film. Matsushita started to offer licenses for production of the VHS player (it was easier to produce than Betamax, which was based on refined technologies by Sony) and positive feedback appeared. Rentals preferred the VHS standard, which was being manufactured by ever more producers and becoming increasingly cheaper. It was also supported by a mass advertisement. Producers of films, whether they wanted to or not, resigned from the preferred videodisc standard and supported VHS, whereas Betamax became marginal and basically reserved for professional use. The story didn't have to turn out this way. Neither Sony nor Matsushita predicted – much the same way others didn't – a fast growth of the rental business and the resulting preference for the cheaper standard. Therefore, as Raynor puts it: 'Matsushita emerged victorious, not because it made *better* choices, but because it happened to have made, for reasons it could not have foreseen, what turned out to be the *right* choices.'[10] It is difficult to judge without knowing in detail the rationality on which Matshushita based its choices. One thing is for sure. The 'hinge' of Matshushita's strategy, which was to assume the key role of low price of the player for customers, turned out to be better than the 'hinge' by Sony, which believed that high technology and high quality were more important.

Making sense of the future in search of strategic 'hinges' is always a game with uncertainty. The simplest and at the same time the most demanding analysis formula has been offered by Jack Welch in form of five open questions, to which the business leaders in GE had to respond on five sheets of paper. It is worth noting that all questions relate to the company's environment – what it is like, how did it change and how can it change in the forthcoming years.[11]

The first question concerns the global dynamics of the market and possible future trends. It is a general question: what is the global market dynamics today, and in what direction will it develop over the next several years? There are certain trends and phenomena concerning almost all companies. Emerging empires like China and India, nationalization of industries like energy raw materials (starting from Russia and ending with Venezuela) or progress of communication technologies, force each leader to think about the consequences of these occurrences because they have a practical meaning for each company. These occurrences change cost structures, market and competition logics, and value chain configurations. It holds true even for institutions like universities, apparently distant from the point of view of market interactions! The growth of China and India provoked a huge expansion of their universities. The quantity and mobility of students and lecturers increased dramatically. Because of new opportunities some scientists with Chinese or Indian origins came back (mainly from the US) to their countries of origin. Possessing resources (in the form of scientists, infrastructure and money), the best Chinese and Indian universities put an emphasis on research and publications. As a result, the number of publications of authors from their universities increased dramatically, which provoked a big competition on the market of publications. It is much more difficult today to publish an article in a prominent scientific journal than it used to be ten years ago. At the same time, progress of communication technologies provoked a completely new potential model of education in the field of management.

Today, every good school of business has a website, on which it puts not only information, but also materials needed for lectures. Some decided to offer free courses online, and some like Harvard Business School, MIT, Berkeley, University of Texas System, Wellesley and Georgetown University created an alliance to develop a new, total online learning model (EdX). This fantastic access to information changes the logics of competition between business schools in a way that is difficult to imagine. On one hand, it forces education institutions to try harder, as standards of excellence, visible thanks to the Internet, constantly rise. On the other hand, it makes every competitive advantage quite transparent and easily imitable. Demographic trends, the progress of technology, the shift of economic importance to Asia, consolidation of many industries by means of mergers and acquisitions are trends, from which it is worth to start an analysis, even in case of a local organization. But in the next step it should obviously be done in more detail by going down to the level of a precise market and industry where the company operates and by seeking one or two phenomena on which to concentrate.

The second and the third questions by Jack Welch concern the history and the environment of the company: what actions have your competitors taken in the last three years to affect this global dynamics? What have you done in the last three years to affect this dynamics? The question concerning the role of competitors is very important, because research and practical experience constantly confirm the thesis that managers tend to have a limited overview of the world surrounding the company. They often don't notice competitors' moves and they are not keen to react to them, unless the implementation of their plan is directly threatened. The question concerning the importance of competitors' activities for the general dynamics of market events is essential. It is well illustrated by the market of daily newspapers and weekly magazines, which is full of turbulence. Both in the US and Europe, newspapers experienced a dramatic crisis, deepened by the economic downturn. Journals go bankrupt and their owners change and consolidate their operations. One of the main reasons for the crisis is the change of the logics of the market, provoked by competitors' activities. Free editions of metropolitan newspapers, news TV channels and live Internet web sites and blogs have deprived daily newspapers of an enormous number of readers. Why buy a newspaper if virtually all the news is obsolete and most texts can be found in the Internet? No wonder that together with the decline in readership, advertisers are leaving newspapers. Even then they constitute the main source of revenue for publishers. However, they are now migrating to the Internet, following readers. Briefly speaking, both general trends and competitors' activities have considerably changed the dynamics and the complexity of the newspaper market, worsening the standing of all companies.

The third question concerns recent company activities and it is as important as the question concerning competitors' activities. Important company activities will have an impact on the immediate environment and it can be both advantageous and dangerous for the company. Coming back to the market of newspapers, almost all newspapers in the world have accelerated the disadvantageous logic of market changes by creating Internet web sites and providing free access to a great quantity of materials from their everyday paper editions. This morning I bought a daily newspaper and later I browsed through its web site. I regretted the purchase, because everything I found interesting had been placed in the Internet for free. Actually, only *The Wall Street Journal* and *The Financial Times* have developed a reasonable policy of paid Internet services within the frame of their strategies – other newspapers in the US and Europe have only worsened the economic situation of the industry through their own actions.

The fourth and the fifth questions by Welch have a retrospective character: what are the most dangerous moves your competitors can make in the next three years in order to affect the industry dynamics? What are the most effective things you could do to bring desirable impact on this dynamics? Both questions make the environment analysis the determinant part and force us to think about our moves and our competitors' moves, as well as their impact on the share of power in the environment. The key to a good analysis is to notice weak signals not noticed by others, the source of changes, which others do not appreciate and to understand the impact of the company's and competitors' actions on the environment. Afterwards managers have to put these together into a logical, simplified map of the future company environment. This will never be complete and perfect and will always constitute a set of hypotheses, which should be periodically verified. Failure to do so will move the company randomly and blindly. Analysis will not be able to define clearly the one or two hinges of a strategy, and therefore won't be able either to define the domain of its operations, nor the type of advantage searched for.

Defining company boundaries – a rule of territory

Company strategy can be effective only within a well-defined territory. There is no strategy and no competitive advantage to a market without boundaries, as nobody can make real sense of the environment on a global scale, in each market segment or referring to each product. A firm cannot develop one global strategy. A model of marketing activities effective in Slovenia or Hungary may not turn out to be successful in Russia or Ukraine – a great surprise to Western investors in the 1990s and even today.

Global luxury products and brands (Prada, Belvedere, Louis Vuitton, Rolex and so on) have their natural boundaries of the segment of cosmopolitan, very wealthy customers, who constitute only a tiny margin of the market – even in the developed world. Mass distribution is economically reasonable only in areas with a high population density (simply speaking – in urban areas). In areas where there are small villages dispersed over a large territory and where people have limited purchasing power (a typical example of Africa and Asia), there is no market for mass distribution. That is why companies like Unilever or P&G in India have developed a model of indirect distribution, using individual entrepreneurs-consultants, and following the pattern of direct distribution of cosmetics producers like Avon or Oriflame. One can multiply examples, but their sense remains the same – strategy requires a thorough definition of the boundaries, a territory of the company's activities, which is understood by managers and on which they are able to develop a simple, coherent competing strategy. Company boundaries are defined by two old strategic questions:

– What is our business and what can it be?
– What is not our business and what it shouldn't be?

Defining boundaries means taking decisions about temporary inclusion and exclusion, which as any other element of strategy, should be periodically verified and discussed because changes in environment or leaders' aspirations can significantly modify the territory of a company's activities.

The strategic domain of the company, or its boundaries in other words, are set by four dynamic dimensions: geography, customers, products and distribution technology (Figure 3.2). The number of issues

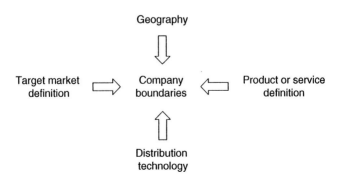

Figure 3.2   Dimensions of an organization's strategic domain

related to these dimensions is quite large, but fortunately, the definition of the strategic domain is made easier because they are not equally important in every company and at any given moment of time. The issues and decisions concerning particular dimensions will be different in big and small companies, based on old and modern technologies, production companies and service companies. For a company considering an internationalization of its operations, the key problem will be to choose the geographic market (e.g. Canada, USA, China, India, developed countries of the UE, new countries of the UE, Ukraine or Russia). Very often, companies have very well-defined markets and products, and their only strategic problem is the distribution technology. There is not a single universal way to define company boundaries. It is always a set of temporary decisions, adapted to a firm's aspirations, resources and capabilities. And it has to occasionally change, sometimes forcing a radical change of strategy and/or business model. A lion moves and fights differently on land than a shark does in water, although their victims might not appreciate that.

Geographic boundaries

The first, and in a way simplest, decision concerns the geographical territory. In spite of all globalization processes, most companies in any economy decide to compete in their original, domestic markets. Most often, the main reason for narrowing company boundaries to the domestic market are limited resources (most small companies are systematically deprived of capital and have a fairly standard offer) and capabilities. Operating outside of the domestic market means transgressing the cultural and institutional distance, bringing new partners with different business practice, different competitors, potentially different customer expectations, changeability of exchange rates and a complicated problem of the transnational supervision of the activities of representation offices, distributors or subsidiaries – briefly speaking a completely different business environment, different costs and a different risk of operations. Therefore, most small and medium companies, consciously or not, limit their operations to domestic markets, minimizing the risk as much as possible. Internationalization operations take place only when it becomes a strategic objective. The most frequent and the oldest reason to extend a geographical boundary is the limit of a domestic market. For example, the company Plastex Composite from Poland, producing professional sports kayaks and canoes (one of the official suppliers of canoes for the Beijing Olympics), had to go international almost immediately after it was born because few people would buy one such product per year in the domestic Polish market. Such an internationalization strategy requires the company to have some particular resources and competences, which are valuable in other markets – unique technologies or unique brands.

Another classic reason to extend boundaries of operations is the search for assets. For hundreds of years companies have acted on an international scale, seeking natural raw materials (from spices, silk and gold to oil) and new products (mainly food, e.g. exotic fruits), which they could not produce in their countries. Thanks to overtaking assets (mines, oil fields, crops), companies acquire control over supplies and prices of raw materials and products, avoiding the possibility of an economic 'blackmail' from exporters.

The third reason to extend company boundaries is the behavior of competitors. This reason is always true in cases of classical oligopolies, when a couple of principal competitors watch each other carefully and mimic each other's strategic moves. It is reasonable behavior, because it does not allow 'escape' from competitors. If internationalization turns out to be an advantageous use of opportunities, all companies make a progress. If it turns out to be a failure – all lose more or less the same. In both cases, the situation of an oligopoly remains stable. Regardless of the reasons of internationalization, it is a fundamental strategic solution with immense consequences – whether the company operates within boundaries of its domestic market or reaches further out.

Market boundaries

The second dimension concerns customers (choice of market segmentation) as well as choice of competitors whom we face in the segments. Let's start with the segmentation from the customers' point of view, because this is the most natural one. The simplest way to define market boundaries is to assess its attractiveness and the possibility of maintaining the advantage over competitors' offers. Therefore, a good manager has to analyze company markets and products constantly as well as seek answers to many questions. What does the value created by our products consist in for customers on a given market? Is it unique? Do customers appreciate this value more than values created by competitors? How will the market evolve? What new events and products will appear on it as weak signals of the forthcoming revolution? What changes in the product/service range are most appreciated by customers? What should the next move of the company be? Should it fight? Or is it perhaps better to wait or exit?

The main question in determining target segments concerns the attractiveness of the given market. Depending on the industry and the strategic concept, managers will apply various criteria. Here are two typical approaches. From the financial perspective, an attractive market is a business area that requires low capital investments, ensures high margins and has a relatively fast pace of growth. Classic examples of such a market would be cosmetics and certain segments of the food industry. From the strategic point of view, an attractive market is big and has a fast pace of growth, whereas competitors have limited possibilities of reacting to our strategic moves. Only the combination of the strategic and the financial aspect of markets correctly define boundaries of the desirable market segment.

Today's powerful market position of the fourth biggest aircraft producer in the world, the Brazilian Embraer, is a result of an unequivocal concentration in mid-1990s on exactly such a market segment. It was a fast-growing market of regional air carriers, which in turn derived from the growth of discount airlines, flying mainly to secondary airports. Embraer focused all its efforts on accomplishing and launching on the market just one product, a 50-passenger aircraft ERJ-145, which was very well adapted to this fast-growing segment of the air transportation market. This move helped the company overtake a large segment of the market previously dominated by Canadian producer Bombardier. The current strategy of Embraer consistently addresses the regional market segment; only the offered aircrafts have become bigger. Interestingly, at the end of the 1990s the decision by Embraer to produce bigger, regional aircrafts (70–110 passengers) was a result of the analysis of the way several airlines in the world were operating. It turned out that in many companies contracts with pilots limited the number of smaller, more economical aircrafts that companies could use. Smaller aircrafts required less experienced pilots who, in turn, were ready to work for less money. That was why pilots' trade unions, defending their wages and influence, have limited the number of smaller aircrafts used by major airlines, forcing air carriers to use big aircrafts on economically non-viable routes. Embraer, taking into account the ever poorer economic performance of airlines, assumed that such a state of affairs would not last forever and therefore started to design new mid-size aircrafts. Thanks to the accumulated financial resources it has survived the market downturn that occurred after 9/11 (Fairchild Dornier has not), and it has successfully launched new aircrafts on the market. Over many years, the careful choice of its domain allowed Embraer to avoid competing with industry's giants. Eventually, this niche has been noticed by leading manufacturers (Boeing and Airbus), who as a result, have introduced some smaller versions of their big aircrafts.[12]

Product and service boundaries

The third dimension of company boundaries is defined by products and services. There is a vast accumulated knowledge in the field of marketing concerning the definition of products. It is common knowledge that it is a complex challenge and that products should be thought of on three levels.[13] The first one is the core product – in essence the answer to the question: what does the customer really buy, what are the benefits he or she gets from the product? The oldest marketing anecdote, which is still worth remembering, says that a customer does not buy drills, but holes. The second level is the real product, that is, the core product enriched with the product's quality, style, brand, packaging and additional features. The third level is the so-called additional product, that is, services and additional benefits accompanying the product. There is a natural tendency, partially forced by the market and competition, to complicate products. For instance, if you buy a Mercedes in Germany, it becomes a ritual. It starts with a complex process of ordering a particular version of the car (and there are hundreds of them), and after a long waiting time comes the ritual of collecting the car at the dealer's or in the manufacturing plant in Stuttgart, where customers are greeted in a special car hall. All these moves add to the product a certain mysticism and enhance its value. The process can also work the other way around as the example of redefinition of products by Gillette at the end of the 1990s shows. Instead of selling shaving razors, the company decided to define its products as 'impulse purchase products' located near cash registers. With such a definition, it started to offer further products (batteries, pens and all other things, which are sold next to a cash register in a supermarket) in order to find new sources of growth. It turned out that there were no expected business synergies in them and a shaving razor didn't – in customers' opinion – constitute an impulse purchase product. The company encountered financial problems and eventually was acquired by Procter & Gamble.

Leaving aside the nuances of marketing enrichment or the definition of products, which can constitute the source of true market innovations, for a strategist it is important to understand the logic of the product's value. It is sometimes nicely called a *value proposition* – what is the real value a customer gets and appreciates.[14] Therefore, managers should consider definitions of the market in terms of how customers define them and what are their needs. It is well illustrated by the great definition of the boundaries of the strategic domain by Edward Jones, a well-known American investment consulting company.

Everybody knows a typical business model of modern company in financial investment business. First, it focuses on rich customers (called HNWI – High Net Worth Individuals), because they have a financial surplus which can be invested. Second, it should offer them a wide *spectrum* of products – from safe ones to complex derivatives – in order to obtain a full range of products and try to maximize the number of products sold to each customer. Third, it should offer them all possible access channels – from individual caretakers to Internet access. Fourth, it should carefully sneak in complex schemes of allowances, operational fees, taxes, interest rates, or high fees, because otherwise customers might feel cheated. It is a fairly coherent and popular strategic model, dominating the market and partially responsible for the financial crisis in 2008. There are also other models, very different but equally coherent, among which the company Edward Jones is an interesting example. It is a medium-sized, but very profitable, intermediary in the field of investments, which attracts the attention of specialists in the field of strategy because of its atypical choices regarding the strategic domain as well as its excellent financial results.[15] The company has an outstanding reputation and has many times won the ranking of *Fortune* for the best employer in the US and Canada.

Edward Jones was founded in 1922 in St. Louis in Missouri as a typical small intermediary in investment banking. Ted Jones, the owner of the company, decided to focus on servicing inhabitants of small towns with the intermediary of one local agent. These were atypical decisions because in such places there aren't many rich people. What is more, one-man offices mean high fixed costs (all costs from rental to telecommunication charged to a single seller). However, the company was growing and in 1967 it already had 62 offices dispersed in the states of the central-west of the US. Its representatives were recruited from local inhabitants and instructed how to establish contacts with local opinion leaders – doctors, tax advisors and lawyers – in a way to become reliable partners. Customers were acquired directly, by door-to-door selling of the product, which even in those times was relatively unusual. First, these were products of the most prestigious and, at best, conservative investment banks, for example, Capital Research, Putnam or Morgan Stanley. Second, these had to be simple and safe products, like for instance shares of solid companies or reliable bonds. The company avoids selling shares, bonds or other financial instruments charged with a high risk, even if the potential revenue could be high. Around 1980, when the company had over 300 offices, it started an expansion to small and medium towns throughout the US as well as Canada and Great Britain. Today, it has over 10,000 offices all over the world and the very same strategy model as 50 years ago: it is a private partnership; it focuses on individual middle-aged customers who worry about their pensions and are risk-averse and search for conservative investments; it sells selected products of prestigious investment banks, which constitute a long-term investment with a relatively secure return on investment. The company's web site informs in detail when actually customers hear from an Edward Jones broker a short 'no' – when they want to buy cheap shares, shares of young (less than ten years) companies, futures and options/derivatives, raw material contracts or other speculative securities. The company unequivocally believes in the philosophy of a traditional, long-term investment and communicates it; it sells through offices served by individual agents, who are partners and not employees of the company; customers can analyze recommendations of Edward Jones on its web page, check their accounts and contact agents by e-mail, though each purchase or sale must be carried out personally. The company doesn't allow customers to make frequent transactions, does not offer online trading or encourage long-term investment perspective.[16] The domain of Edward Jones, in particular, clearly defines the type of served customers – conservative, long-term investors taking their decisions with help of reliable advisors. Products and location are attuned precisely to the needs of customers. Additionally, the company's boundaries are defined by conscious decisions to focus on locations in small and medium towns, conservative products of the best providers (the company doesn't actually create products it sells) and personal service.

Boundaries of distribution technologies

The last element of the company's boundaries is the technology of delivering products and services to the given market. While developing a strategy, it is important not to treat technology as a given, but as a choice, because this often allows for true innovations exemplified by personalized service system of Edward Jones, TV channels like BBC or CNN, Internet consulting or education, mega shops by Zara, air transportation of packages by FedEx, TNT or DHL. Distribution technology is a very important and often underestimated strategic element of company boundaries. In the shadow of the spectacular success of products such as iPod, iPhone and iPad by Apple, not many people have noticed very important strategic decisions concerning the distribution, which have given the company an opportunity to appropriate margins created by these new products. One of Steve Jobs' crucial decisions in 1990s concerned a total change of the distribution system. Jobs resigned from thousands of contracts with smaller electronic shops and established contracts with big networks instead and started – for the first time in the company's history – its own Internet sales. He also took a then-controversial (and expensive) decision to build his own network of mega shops. In such a way, he extended the value chain of Apple and started to control distribution and retail.[17] It was a strategic decision and the right decision, because the demand for iPods ensured a huge inflow of customers coming to brand shops while at the same time increasing sales of other products – computers, phones and hardware devices.

Belle International, the world's biggest producer of women's shoes, started its production together with thousands of other producers in China. One of Belle's most important strategic decisions in the 1990s was to concentrate its investments on the sales network by establishing its own shops, but also – which was then a true innovation – by arranging its own open stands in a new distribution channel – shopping malls. Belle worked in a systemic way – it enlarged its area to all of China, created new brands of women's shoes and set up separate stands for each brand. In such a way, it decreased its costs of entering this key distribution channel, at the same time blocking space for competitors in the fastest-growing distribution channel in China.[18]

Defining a company's boundaries is a difficult process, and a conscious limitation of domain seems sometimes to be against the company's best interest. Let's have a look at the example of listed company K2 – Poland's 'hidden champion' of e-marketing. K2 very precisely defined its area of activities in e-marketing, and for a long time was developing competences only in this field, consciously limiting its domain and its dynamics of growth. The company's leaders recall that paradoxically this was one of their most difficult decisions as the demand for other Internet services was huge. As they said, 'you could put an "e-" before any noun and create a new field of activity'.[19] Internet was growing very dynamically and its applications had multiplied. Many e-marketing agencies got caught in this trap and spread their resources thinly, constantly expanding their field of activity. Creating software and technological solutions complementing e-marketing projects seemed to be particularly natural. K2, as well, ventured for a moment into peripheral e-mail marketing services and lost quite a lot of money. However, mangers quickly recognized their mistake and concentrated only on e-marketing, without being tempted to expand scope of the firm's activities. The leaders of K2 credit this specialization as enabling the company to become the industry leader in Poland.

It is very difficult to define boundaries of a big, multiproduct company operating in many markets, but it is always a fascinating cognitive process. The change of boundaries or their definition leads sometimes to a completely new approach to business and to the opportunity to question the existing solutions as well as to reconsider all existing choices. But the basis of this process always comes back to the two questions mentioned at the beginning: what is our business and what can it be? What is not our business and what shouldn't it be? As A.G. Lafley, former CEO of Procter & Gamble, underlines, and rightly so, the second question is more difficult and 'only the CEO has the enterprise-wide perspective to make these tough choices, because although most business leaders are motivated by growth opportunities, they find it exceedingly hard to recommend shutting down or selling a business they're a part of. (...) Determining which businesses we should not be in is an on-going effort that calls for continual pruning and weeding. Disposing of assets is not as sexy as acquiring them, but it's just as important'.[20]

During discussing of the above process of setting boundaries, I only accidentally mentioned an aspect that is in fact very important from the strategic decision-making point of view – competitors. The choice of market and products equals the choice of competitors – and this is better as a conscious choice rather than a random one. This is well illustrated by the example of Kooperacja Techniczna, a Polish entrepreneurial firm. This company created and patented a new type of dryer for 3-D glasses, which surely after the popularity of the movie, *Avatar*, came to be used increasingly often in theaters playing 3-D movies. Their dryers are much cheaper and faster than the previous models. Now the question arises, what are the boundaries of the market? Most Polish cinemas are not independent but are part of cinema chains, meaning that you need to define the whole country as your market. But every analysis will show you that the Polish market of such devices, having a life cycle of a couple of years, is easily saturated, which in turn means the end of operations. An additional complication, but also an additional opportunity, is that a part of networks is international, and their suppliers as well. This means that when entering a market our producer almost automatically deals with competitors. Even patents protecting devices will not stop global suppliers from imitating or avoiding patents in the long run. This is why from the very beginning the Polish entrepreneur has to think about his territory at least on a regional scale (Europe), because after catering to the Polish market it will face the European market, which is occupied by bigger players.

What should the market and product definition be? Different market definitions in the strategy of our producer of dryers may provoke a clash with various competitors. How should this firm define the market? If it defines it as a set of cinema networks, will it narrow the set of customers since the dryer could potentially find applications outside of the cinema market?

How should it define its product? Simply speaking, it is an industrial washer and dryer, but what features of this product are the most important for a network customer – reliability, speed, price, durability, service warranty? Or maybe customers are actually mainly interested in outsourcing the whole process, since purchasing machines means the acquisition and maintenance of additional assets and potentially the need to hire additional workers. In this case, the chain of cinemas would be probably ready to buy the glass-drying service. This would mean a different definition of the product and a different way of delivering it. In case of such an operating model, competitors are suppliers of services and specialists in outsourcing (like Impel), as opposed to producers of cinema equipment.

This leads us to another issue, namely the way of delivering products or services to a given market and geographical area. Should the company deliver the product by itself or should it hire an external distribution network? How will it deliver if it is supposed to do so on its own? Via Internet, a network of sales representatives or in yet another way? Each of these solutions has different competitive consequences. Development of a distribution network means increasing costs and a long time for development, but in return it offers control over the selling process and a constant possibility to gather information about the market. Thanks to this, a firm can develop a better map of the environment and obtain fast information about competitors' moves. An external distribution network allows the reach of a significantly bigger market almost immediately, but it is usually much more expensive in the short term and means a lack of deep understanding and information about the market. It results in great difficulties (described in the theory of economy and well known in practice) with building such a system of incentives, which will effectively motivate the distribution network to perform two or more tasks simultaneously. If it is not a network dedicated to one product and one producer, it is impossible to build such an effective system.[21] The network concentrates on the task, from which it will have the greatest benefits, which will certainly be selling and not monitoring competition. Sales can grow, but the producer becomes almost blind and deaf to potential competitive threats in the environment.

Discipline in the choice of territory means therefore a thorough analysis and conscious choices on the junction of the market definitions from the point of view of customers and competitors. If a market is attractive to us, it can also be attractive to competitors. That is why if we decide to build a position on a given territory, a strategist must estimate potential moves of competitors from the point of view of two criteria: competitors' readiness to react to our moves and the strength of this reaction. Simply speaking, if the territory on which we want to fight is important also for the competitor, we can expect that he or she will take up a fight. If the competitor has a big market share, considerable resources and capabilities and is emotionally attached to the market, we are taking a high risk entering this territory. If so far network cinemas are equipped with dryers by a specialized Western manufacturer, it will most probably react aggressively toward any entrant. For the competitor, the entry of the Polish manufacturer will constitute a 'to be or not to be' issue. The smaller the stake and the capabilities of the new competitor, the bigger the chance that the established company will leave the competitor alone. Thus, if dryers are delivered by a manufacturer for whom this particular market is one of many in which they operate, or if it is only a marginal market niche, one can expect to occupy this market before the established company actually decides how to react. The risk of such an entry strategy is minimal.

Above all, a strategically good choice of territory should not antagonize competitors, or it should at least make it difficult for them to react effectively. It is easier said than done, but leaders have a couple of simple tools to implement such strategies. They can determine geographical boundaries in a way to maintain a beachhead on the competitor's main market in order to merely observe its moves, but without provoking any reaction. At the same time, such a move is a classic signal that if the competitor attacks our key geographical market, it can immediately expect payback on its market. Such a strategy of 'mutual observation points' often stabilizes competition and permits conduct of the strategy on one's own market calmly and with discipline.

A second way is an innovative, or simply different, definition of segments and products, which means avoiding competing in the same segment as the strongest competitors. Japanese companies have used this approach for many years entering or creating low segments of the car and motorcycle market, as well as the market of electronic devices, carefully avoiding direct competition, until they felt sufficiently strong and experienced. These same strategies have been applied by Central European companies wanting to enter world markets after first attempts to compete directly proved unsuccessful. Today, they are also applied by Indian and Chinese companies, both in developed markets and their own. A model example are Chinese car companies, who already dominated low segments of their domestic market, but who are quickly improving their cars, thanks to purchases of technologies and brands from declining giants. The biggest private manufacturer, Geely Holding Group Co., prepared six new platforms for 2009, eight by the end of 2010 and altogether over 40 new models are slated by the end of 2015. They bought an Australian producer of gear boxes and transmission gears and Volvo, announcing at the same time a very ambitious plan to compete in all segments. They have also overtaken production of London cabs, but in practice for the time being they are focusing on lower and medium segments of the Chinese market.

Cherry Automobile successfully develops the market of small, economical and cheap Chinese cars. Weichi Power, a manufacturer of diesel motors, has bought a French producer of such motors. BYD has produced a mass electric car. And one cannot forget about Indian Tata Motors, which not only produces Nano, the cheapest car in the world (the verdict if it is a success or a failure still is in the air but it has already stirred similar moves by other producers), but has also bought Jaguar and Land Rover. The second biggest Indian car producer Bajaj Auto envied Tata Motors and its success with Nano, and decided in November 2009 to produce an even cheaper car jointly with Nissan and Renault. Differences between the partners on design and pricing eventually led Bajaj Auto to launch in January 2012 its own version of low cost mini car 'RE60'. If Chinese and Indian manufacturers implement their strategies for ultra-low-cost cars successfully, they will dominate the world low-market segments. Having economies of scale incomparable with any other producer, they can effectively climb the ladder of market segments – with time and systematic learning.

The third way to avoid direct competition is a different technology of delivering products to customers, in other words a different model of distribution and/or sales. A classic example of this strategy would obviously be companies selling directly, such as Avon, Oriflame or Mary Kay Cosmetics, who have built their beauty care empires by reaching customers directly with help of armies of locally operating salespersons. In computer games, online gaming is a very dynamic market (MMORPGs – *multiplayer online role-playing games*), thanks to the distribution and participation via Internet, effectively allowing them to avoid the issue of piracy. Hilti, a tool manufacturer from Lichtenstein, shot ahead of competitors thanks to a radical change in its operations' technology, which transformed products into services. Instead of selling tools, it started to rent them to construction and assembly companies via a system called *Fleet Management*. Over 60,000 companies worldwide pay Hilti a monthly fee and can use any tools that Hilti not only delivers but also maintains and insures against theft.[22] The above example of outsourcing the drying of glasses in cinemas instead of selling dryers is also a classic example of avoiding competition in this field. Geography, segmentation of customers and technology create many opportunities to avoid direct confrontation with competitors. In practice, managers often forget this and provoke competitors to react. Of course, you can provoke competitors all you want – but it is best when it is actually one of the objectives of your strategy.

4
Discipline of Strategy Execution: Goals and Business Model

Where do goals come from?

If we look carefully at the ways organizations define and try to achieve goals, many of them would be better suited as units of analysis in the theory of catastrophes rather than the theory of strategy. Managers frequently formulate unclear, nonmeasurable and conflicting goals, and then modify them during the implementation phase in order to match results. However, this practice doesn't change the fact that when speaking about management in general, and in particular about strategic management, we are talking about a goal-oriented activity, which should, by nature, be on the opposite end of the spectrum from randomness and should preclude meandering away from once-set objectives. But where do organizational goals come from? Let's start with a short theoretical background, which will allow us to better understand a good practice of formulating strategic goals, and then we'll move on to practical directives, which are necessary in the discipline of the strategy's implementation.

In theory, we distinguish three approaches to the issue of strategic organizational goals: normative, systemic and behavioral. The normative approach, characteristic of the classic theory of organization and neoliberal economy, assumes that a company is (or more correctly speaking – should be) a tool, a metaphoric engine to achieve goals, which emerges from the logic of the market system. A clearly defined basic goal – achieving profit for the shareholders – is the company priority. It was most sharply repeated in 1970 by the Nobel Prize winner M. Friedman in his article titled provocatively 'The Social Responsibility of a Company is to Increase its Profit'. In his opinion (first expressed in his book *Capitalism and Freedom*), 'there is one and only one social responsibility of business – to use its resources and engage in activities designed to increase its profits so long as it stays within the rules of the game, which is to say, engages in open and free competition without deception or fraud.'[1] This controversial – to say the least – opinion gained many followers in the 1980s and 1990s, and they do have good arguments. First, it conforms to the logic of a market economy in its simplest version. We can only optimize the state of one variable – the remaining goals can logically play the role of constraints. So if we treat the assumptions of the market economy concerning private ownership and the role of competition as fundamental, the company should optimize its function of effectiveness by maximizing profit and long-term dividends for shareholders. Other goals (customer satisfaction, employee satisfaction, respect for law, social responsibility etc.) constitute nothing but constraints to this process. Second, if the company should simultaneously seek to achieve other goals apart from maximizing profit, behaving in a socially responsible way would theoretically be advantageous for everyone. However in practice, it could mean greater costs and uncertainty for the company itself.[2]

Let's look at the simplest example – a food producer who, apart from wanting to make profits, also decides to behave in a socially responsible fashion by exclusively producing ecological food from the best raw materials. As a result of this decision, it will have the highest variable costs in the industry (expensive raw materials), and at the same time will operate in conditions of great uncertainty concerning customer behavior. Although most consumers support the idea of healthy food and ingredients of the highest quality, only some are keen to pay a high price for them. In the situation of an economic downturn where customers are in money-saving mode, though most every customer will still support the concept of healthy, ecological and organic food, they are more likely to buy cheaper products promoted on special offers in supermarkets. This is a normal and reasonable behavior, however it globally creates what in game theory is called 'an unstable equilibrium', on which the company should not develop its strategy.

Finally, the third argument – the normative goal of maximizing profits – argues that companies should neither achieve goals nor perform activities that are outside of direct function of the company, as this leads to bad allocation of resources and decreased effectiveness. Arguments of adversaries of this extreme opinion by Friedman have always concerned basic assumptions related to the logic of market economy. But only the latest global crisis added a true weight to these arguments, because it questioned the assumption concerning the effective market functioning, the competition and the only legitimate goal of creating value for shareholders. In practice, the market is a lazy, shabby, morally indifferent mechanism, which is only effective in the long run. What the 'long run' actually means nobody really knows. Therefore, dragging on the time perspective as an argument in favor of the effectiveness of the market does not clarify much and does not contribute a lot to the theory of goals of an enterprise.

A completely different view on the issue of organizational goals is the systems approach, which was developed in parallel with economics and theory of organizations.[3] It is important for a totally new understanding of the essence of the organizational goal category. It focuses on the category of survival as a primary goal of each system. Every system can be described with a set of essential variables whose values determine its survival. Using the concept of essential variables allows us to define the differences between the processes of controlling and regulating, which are a systemic equivalent of the process of management. Controlling consists in determining intervals of acceptable values of essential variables and regulating means maintaining values of these variables within the determined intervals. The quality criterion applied in the cybernetic regulation is extremely conservative – survival of the system. Looking at management from the cybernetic perspective, it is a set of decisions and actions restoring a balance in organizations, defined by a set of important variables (or goals) and intervals of values, in which they should be maintained. It is a complex and dynamic process because the balance is constantly disturbed by occurrences taking place in either environment or internal disturbances. From this perspective, a real strategic challenge is an understanding of which variables are essential, in which intervals they should be maintained, and how to do it in the face of constant disruptions.[4] Equilibrium, at the very least, ensures the company's survival, and at best ensures adaptation and progress.

The last theoretical approach deserving particular attention is the behavioral approach. It was built on the grounds of the theory of organization in the1960s and was rediscovered by economists 30 years later in the form of the modern 'behavioral economics'. What is important in the behavioral approach is that from the very beginning it has questioned the thesis of the clarity of a company's goal(s), not so much on the grounds of axiological arguments, but rather repetitive results of research studies. For several years studies have indicated that goals of organizations are multiple, unclear and contradictory, whereas relations between goals, means and participants' behaviors are vague and distinguishing between goals and means can be difficult.[5] If we treat an organization as the behavioral approach does, which is as a social and technical system, it is obvious that in order to survive, the system has to implement a set of goals satisfying expectations of various stakeholders. It is a concept similar to the cybernetic category of 'important variables', and was adopted by H. Simon, who formulated a simple concept of a company goal. He proposed to treat the goal as a set (a 'tunnel') of limitations, within which the organization is free to choose its main goal. The choice of one of these limitations as the main goal of activity results from the organizational structure. Speaking more simply, it is a decision of the top management.[6]

All three theories of organizational goals are important because they allow us to better understand the dilemmas in formulating strategic goals. Should there be one goal or many? Should the main goal be the value created for shareholders or should the company be socially responsible and care about how its objectives fit into the vision, mission and so on? As I previously said, the condition of simplifying strategy requires establishing unambiguous goals and an understanding of the necessity to clearly formulate limiting conditions, which should be met by the company in order to survive. Of course, the company must be profitable; it must meet minimum expectations of suppliers, customers and employees; it must act in conformity with law and clearly assess the level of various kinds of risk that it can withstand and accept. The role of leaders is to specify the minimum level of each of these limitations and to create such a formula of management – using, for example, as a tool the popular, balanced scorecard by Kaplan and Norton, which can make the organization effective within these limitations.[7] Moving from theoretical to practical examples: Ryanair, as a profitable airline, treats the safe, predictable air transportation from A to B as its main limiting condition. The quality of service is neither the goal nor the priority – passengers must quickly climb the steps to the aircraft, take unnumbered seats and accept the lack of any service during the flight. As the boss of the airline, M. O'Leary, says, 'We clearly communicate our rules to passengers. You won't get free food. We don't want you to take luggage. And we won't pay you for a hotel just because you grandma has died.'[8] And the reaction of passengers is reasonable – they don't have any special expectations apart from safety and timeliness of the flight, because the company unequivocally defines 'service quality' as transport from one place to another within a determined time. End of story.

Judging from the actions and decisions of managers, Ryanair has had two strategic goals for years – maximization of profit and growth. It is worth noticing that these goals must be conflicting from time to time! Increases in the prices of fuel in 2007 and 2008 significantly decreased the company's profit (costs of fuel increased from roughly 30% of operational costs to 50%), and the simplest way to defend profitability would have been to slow down growth. Instead, Ryanair demonstrated that it considers growth to be the main strategic goal through the purchase of new aircrafts, the launching of new destinations (only in 2008 Ryanair launched about 220 new routes, in 2010 it was about 360 new routes, and in 2011 about 200!), and by constantly decreasing flight fares. By doing this, they settled on lower profitability in the short – or even medium – run.

Strategic goals – a rule of minimum

While formulating strategic goals, the rule of minimum should be respected. There should only be one goal, which should be clearly defined (measurable), ambitious and should be achievable within a set period of time. The role of leaders is to overcome organizational games, navigate a maze of interests and expectations and extinguish the natural temptation to simultaneously follow diverse directions. Strategic goals should be one at a time because a firm can only follow one direction. The strategic goal can be pace of growth, market share, profit, share value, cash flow, product innovations, alliances, employee or customer satisfaction. It can even be excellence (on the condition we can quantify 'excellence' for the benefit of management). This was the case with Indian conglomerate Bharti, which defined the goal as follows: 'until the year 2020 we will make Bharti the best Indian conglomerate'. The already-mentioned Galanz has had a consistent strategic goal over many years – the biggest share in the Chinese (and today global) market of microwaves. It achieved this goal through alliances with a growing number of companies, for which it was producing as an OEM, and growth of production scale as well as through regular price wars eliminating smaller competitors. From 1995 to 2005, it reduced prices on the Chinese market nine times. It started its first great war against Korean conglomerate LG, the market leader in China, in October 1997 by reducing all prices by 40 percent. Then came other reductions aimed at the industry's consolidation. When it reached a scale of production of 1.25 million pieces, it reduced all its prices to the average cost of a company with a production capacity of 800,000 pieces. When it exceeded the scale of four million pieces, it decreased the prices to the level of the average cost of a company producing two million, and by the scale of ten million it repeated the same operation assuming five million pieces as a break point.[9]

One can also imagine the case of the two basic strategic goals since in such a case you can still clearly say what their hierarchy is. This is what Honda did; they conquered the American market with its motorcycles in the 1960s by formulating two long-term strategic goals – growth of sales and profitability. They had a clear hierarchy – the rate of growth of sales was a priority (measured by the number of sold motorcycles), profitability was the second goal. Galanz, after achieving the dominating position on the global market of microwaves, enlarged its production profile and had two strategic goals: maintaining the leading position on the market of microwaves based on innovations and maximizing market share.

The problem arises when there are too many strategic goals, very frequent in management practice. This creates the difficult necessity of having to define a hierarchy of goals in a clear way. Problems will inevitably arise in terms of mutual coherence and transferability – in extreme cases, goal one is at a given moment of time more important than goal two and goal two more important than goal three, but within a given period of time, goal three might be more important than goal one and so on. This also leaves space for all sorts of games for power, influence and resources. The strategic position is only clear in the case of designating one or two superior goals, and treating other 'goals' more as important limitations, which should be analyzed and monitored (as all three presented organizational theories suggest, starting however from different points of departure). The definition of such strategic goals belongs to leaders and should be well rooted in the situational overview of the particular company taking into consideration the business environment and company's boundaries. In this sense, it is not a free choice because it must be well justified. However, this doesn't mean that it must automatically be accepted by owners and/or investors. If they decide that a given choice is wrong, they can either change the board of management or decide to manage themselves.

The goal should be clearly formulated, because only then will it be truly measurable. The best way to formulate the goal precisely is to give it a character of an important ratio. Market share alone, profit alone or the number of new products alone don't say much about the company, but the ratio, for example between the market share and the pace of market growth or between the market share and the market share of the main competitor, is a precise strategic measure of the pace of growth. Based on research, Jim Collins paid particular attention to the importance of such goals and underlined that some companies concentrated their whole attention on one single indicator which they considered to be an essential measure of their strategy.[10] For instance, steel producer, Nucor, monitors the index of profit per one ton of steel, retailer Wal-Mart monitors sales per one meter of store surface and Elektrobudowa, a huge Polish company in industrial construction, strives for maximization of dividend paid to owners. Each company should find its own way of measurement, which will constitute a compass constantly reminding what the essence of the strategic goal is.

The goal must be set within a specific time frame. The decision concerning the time horizon is one of the most important, yet neglected, solutions when developing strategy. Regardless of whether it is a stock-exchange listed company or not, the success of the company cannot be postponed to an undetermined future. The problem of building the company's future without completely sacrificing the present results (which you mustn't do, as it is a condition actually limiting survival) is one of the key dilemmas of strategic management. Companies trying to solve this dilemma often opt for extremities. The first case is an extreme prolongation of time frame that makes the distribution of forecasted results to resemble a hockey stick – the first years are the time of investment, which equate to a loss of (or zero) profit and a negative cash flow, and only in the later future appears a promise of a slow return from investment and a great profit. The problem with such a concept of time period is that, first of all, you don't know whether this promise comes true, and second you don't know how to finance the company's operations in the period of striving toward future profitability.

The second extremity is equally frequent in practice. Boards of management focus on one strategic goal in a short term, because this is when they can achieve excellent results relatively quickly, for example, financial results, by undertaking risky decisions promoting sales, selling company assets, reducing employment, saving on research and development and new implementations. Outstanding quarterly results thwart people from noticing the anorectic character of the company's operations, allowing it to 'eat up' its own future.

There is no easy solution to this problem. In management practice, this typically appears as a dilemma of the 'either-or' type, whereas it should rather be perceived as a necessity of the 'and-and' type. It is obvious that the longer the time frame, the naturally bigger the uncertainty and variability of the environment, as well as expected results. The shorter the time frame, the more predictable the results, but the smaller the scale of activities and quantifiable changes in the company's operations, which can define its long-term future. Each company should search for its own definition of a good time horizon somewhere between these two extremes. Sometimes the dilemma of choice is best solved by accepting the standard. A typical standard was commonly defined as a period of five years. Its genesis lay in a typical cycle of investment, which in heavy industry lasted five years. Today, neither the stock exchange quarterly standard, the financial annual standard nor the five-year standard is binding and well justified for all. That is why company leaders can and should consistently take decisions concerning the optimal time frame at a given moment of time from the point of view of a strategy – should it be one year, two years, three years, four, five, seven, ten years or more. It is a typical 'outside-in' decision, because it mainly depends on environmental conditions. An intensive attack from competitors, a distribution consolidation, an increase of mass sales channels in the form of hypermarkets naturally forces producers of food or beverages to shorten the time horizon of their strategies. A typical three-year economic cycle in the chemical industry imposes a natural three to six-year horizon of thinking. National Forests in most of the countries treat the period of ten years as a tactical time frame and the period of a hundred years as a strategic time frame because that what it takes to grow a tree.

The decision on the assumed time frame is not irrevocable. Sometimes, the business environment changes almost radically because of one important and difficult (or impossible to predict) event, which breaks previous trends. The oil crisis in the 1970s, the terrorist attack on 9/11 in the USA, or the collapse of Lehman Brothers and the global economic downturn in 2008 have all required an immediate reaction. In most cases, it would have been absurd to continue the former strategy without conducting a new thorough analysis of the environment and checking whether the new situation requires any change of the company's boundaries or of the company's strategic goal and – most often – a shortening of its time frame. What is really important is that the decision on the strategic goal's time frame is always an independent decision of leaders responsible for the company's strategy. Its essence is a product of the natural contradiction built into this situation. It is a contradiction between searching for a maximum control over the fate of the company in the short run and a natural fear of potential effects of uncertainty related to long-term trends in the environment, as well as unexpected events, which influence the company's operations.

The goal must be ambitious, yet achievable. In the last 20 years, the idea of setting very ambitious goals has become very popular and has appeared in various forms. Two gurus of management, Hamel and

Prahalad, argued in 1990 that companies must formulate great strategic intentions, because these great strategic intentions constitute a sign of good management and only they are proper for great business leaders.[11] Jim Collins and Jerry Porras supported them with their BHAGs concept (*Big, Hairy, Audacious Goals*), that is very risky and ambitious super goals as a new good standard in management.[12] New language and new ways of thinking about strategic goals have been created. They have been translated into practice by the icon of the contemporary modern management, the globally imitated company General Electric, with its slogan raised by the CEO Jack Welch to the level of a fundamental strategic goal – 'Number 1 or 2 on each global market.' This trend has also reached emerging economies. In the research on dominant logics (cognitive maps) of entrepreneurs in transitional markets researchers found that market leaders could be distinguished from average companies thanks to much bigger ambitions, optimism in perceiving the environment, treatment of competition as a challenge rather than a threat, greater readiness and belief in ability to influence the company's future.[13]

In spite of the intuitive obviousness of the idea of such ambitious goals (it is difficult to jump high when the crossbar is low), it is a dangerous way of thinking and strategizing. Setting ambitious or super ambitious goals, encouraged by theorists and gurus of management, means in practice undertaking great risks and managing on the edge.[14] The effects can be painfully obvious, as we see thanks to the recent global crisis. There is no possibility for each company to be number one on the market and for each product to have a profitability from the upper quartile. It simply contradicts the logics of statistical distribution, which says that most companies must have average results. In the meantime, the theory of management shaped by 'gurus' inspired companies to set extremely ambitious challenges. Shareholders added an additional impulse for acceptance of an ever higher level of risk, treating companies as a mechanism of creating value and linking managers' pay to share value. Finally, an additional (even if temporary) prize for undertaking such risks is the winning managers' celebrity status. Supervisory boards around the world were ready to pay managers with star status exorbitant salaries, not to mention generous options. In exchange for giant pay and bonuses, shareholders and supervisory boards expected stable and high results and constant growth. And managers were producing these results – at the cost of undertaking risks, best illustrated by the example of the level of leverage of Lehman Brothers. At the end of 2007 the company had over 22 billion dollars of equity and 691 billion dollars in assets. This means 669 billion dollars' worth of assets were actually financed with debt!

We are our own worst enemies. There are guilty people all around us – among politicians, economists, managers, theorists in management and consultants. These people have created totally unrealistic expectations as far market possibilities of a normal company are concerned. They have also created an unrealistic concept of strategic goals, ironically described by L. Bossidy and R. Charan in their book on the execution of strategy: 'Your boss has asked you to drive from Chicago to Oskaloosa, Iowa, a journey of 317 miles. He's prepared a budget for you with clear metrics. You can spend no more than 16 dollars on gas, you must arrive in 5 hours and 37 minutes, and you can't drive over 60 miles per hour. But no one has a map to Oskaloosa, and you don't know whether you'll run into a snowstorm on the way.'[15]

Without any doubt, the goal is very ambitious and demanding, the limitations clear, but the whole concept of such an action doesn't make sense. Therefore, it is worth reconstructing our idea of strategic goals. The view that goals should be ambitious but realistic seems to me the most reasonable way of thinking. There is no 'rocket science' of such goal setting. A good analysis of the environment linked to a realistic judgment of organizational competences and resources must be sufficient substance to take decisions. Ram Charan is right in advising company leaders as follows: 'Stretched goals can fire up people's imagination and bring energy to the organization, but only when they are doable. The point is not to get people to work harder. Rather, it is to get people to do things differently and thus raise the capability of the organization. Such a goal carries with it higher risks. Unless you do the mental gymnastics necessary to figure out what has to radically change, setting a stretch goal won't be credible and the organization won't trust you. You have to make sure that people are prepared to think differently and have sufficient resource to accomplish the goals.'[16]

Complementing strategic goals with priorities

Natural complements to strategic goal are clear priorities of activities within a given time. Goals are long or medium term, and they indicate the general direction the company is heading. Priorities concern all the most important undertakings in a given time, as well as the most important activities and resource allocations with regard to these undertakings. An organization constantly faces a flood of tasks, challenges, threats and opportunities. Almost every day, there are important and urgent events. A main customer cancels orders, production manufactures a series of faulty products, trade unions announce a strike in one of the factories, and the government has suddenly changed the regulations. The landscape on which the organization operates is constantly moving, and micro-turbulences are a norm. There is a huge natural temptation, or even a psychological imperative, to react to all of these turbulences, almost endlessly absorbing the attention of managers. As a result, there are endless meetings, hundreds of daily e-mails, new programs for action and a constant feeling of needing to catch up. It requires constant decision-making in a company. And it must be this way. However, the only way to prevent managers, the company in general, from drowning in the flood of everyday problems and decisions and to make them keep strategic goals in mind is to set priorities in a clear way. Priorities define activities, which are most important from the point of view of strategic goals, and are unequivocally linked to the allocation of key resources; typical decisions concern urgent matters and regulate current problems. Most organizations and leaders have trouble setting clear priorities, even when they are able to formulate a precise strategy. We can see this like in a lens through the following example.

Not so long ago, I was leading a workshop in strategic management for managers from an administration in one of the big European cities. The city had defined a strategy in conformity with good, well-grounded principles. Methodologically, it all looked quite nice. They had conducted an analysis of strengths and weaknesses of the town, as well as of the threats and opportunities the town was facing. They had formulated a long-term vision, mission and three main strategic goals. The problem was that they had proposed several measures for each goal. This obviously served a political purpose because by manipulating indices, you can always prove that a given goal has been effectively achieved to a high degree. However, it doesn't help the actual implementation of the strategy. It became even more complex because each of the strategic goals had been additionally divided into operational goals. The cascade of goals wouldn't have been such a problem if the strategy hadn't comprised of over 70 programs and plans for action, each somehow connected to operational goals. Behind each program there was actually a manager taking decisions, employees involved and groups of stakeholders fighting for the limited resources of the city. Of course, each of these programs and projects was reasonable; each of them was probably necessary and lay within the duties or capabilities of the city. However, any attempt to treat 70 programs as a priority is a recipe for disaster. It means dispersing key resources (money and the best people), lack of common time frame (programs have different time frames for implementation and various degrees of complexity), as well as an absolute lack of leaders' focus. Therefore, the city in developing its strategy had to answer the difficult question: what are our main goals, and which programs should become our priority.

A good pattern of the process of defining priorities is the strategic experience of General Electric. Each of its consecutive CEOs faced the challenge of managing probably the biggest, most diversified and complex conglomerate in the world. When Jack Welch took over the position of CEO in the 1980s, he stated that it was a too-complex organization to create a single strategy. However, this didn't prevent him later from indicating unequivocal strategic goals and priorities for action for all managers.[17] In the first period (1984–8) leaders defined three main domains of GE: service, high technologies and core activities (technical equipment, locomotives, turbines, lighting etc., which constituted the traditional business of GE). The common strategic goal for each particular company (division) within GE was to occupy the first or second position in their local domain. Three priorities derived from this goal concerned investments and operations of the whole company. Companies in services were supposed to make acquisitions, companies in high technologies to invest in research and development and companies in traditional domains to improve productivity and quality. The second priority was to achieve leading market position and high return on capital fast. If the company had real problems with these priorities, it was restructured, closed down or sold. The third priority was to accelerate and deformalize the process of taking decisions by means of a radical simplification of the structure (five out of nine managerial levels were eliminated).

In the second period (1988–92) the company concentrated on two strategic goals: globalization of operation and development of an organizational culture rooted in three values – speed, simplicity and self-confidence. Four issues became a priority. The first priority was to build the organizational culture by leveraging the famous *Work-Outs*, which were meetings of employees from various plants, during which they worked out hundreds of improvements and changes. The second priority was to further develop GE's own school of management in Crotonville NY and a mass, complex curriculum for training leaders acting in conformity with the new norms of the GE culture. The third priority was the program *Best Practices*, which aimed at learning new methods and techniques of management from the best firms in the world. The fourth priority was to acquire firms overseas, especially in areas where the position of GE was weak – that is, Asia, Latin America and Central Europe. In the third period (the 1990s), fundamental goals didn't change, but three different programs became priority: becoming a company without boundaries (internal transfer of knowledge and the best management practices), developing new services (also by traditional businesses by complementing products with services) and radically improving quality by applying *Six Sigma*.

The policy of J. Welch is being continued by his successor Jeff Immelt, who has set the speed of organic growth of sales equaling 8 percent (excluding mergers and acquisitions) as one of strategic goals. Since it is virtually impossible to achieve such a goal on stagnating Western markets, Immelt has indicated investments on emerging markets (especially China and India) as the first company priority, assuming that over 60 percent of organic growth would come from them. The second natural priority was to concentrate investments on infrastructural products and technologies (turbines, water purification, railway and air transportation), which are most important in those markets. The third priority was to invest in development of renewable green technologies, which give an opportunity for long-term growth on mature markets. Each of these priorities actually meant changes in the process of allocating resources within GE, as well as in the systems of human management.

It is worth underlining that neither during the times of J. Welch, nor J. Immelt, was it always possible to achieve ambitious strategic goals, but they are both masters of explicit formulation of priorities, indispensable in achieving these goals. The most common managerial mistake in the process of strategy development is lack of focus resulting from too many goals and priorities in a given time. The true role of leaders in such situations is to take difficult decisions concerning concentration of efforts and resources and to be able to say 'no' to programs and initiatives. This is very difficult in practice because nobody likes to take decisions which end financing of certain activities or important programs. Each company product, program or activity, considered individually, always finds a good justification to be funded. Even those programs, which at a given moment of time create mostly problems and do not give good prognoses for the future, are usually defended with arguments claiming that more resources and more commitment will eventually contribute to their success in the future. Another traditional argument consists of referring to expenditures incurred in the past. The longer the history of a given project and the greater the commitment of resources into it, the more difficult it is (as the RISC project in Intel discussed later shows) – to stop it or to take resources away from it. It makes sense in such a situation to accept a position natural for economists – that the costs incurred are sunken costs and do not constitute support for a new budget expenditure.

Decisions on priorities are always directly or indirectly related to decisions concerning allocation of resources and cutting down budgets or shutting down ongoing projects These are extremely unpopular decisions, which evoke protests or even aggression, create conflicts and are difficult to be implemented. I remember when a president from one Central European university asked me for advice concerning setting priorities for his mandate, I asked him about his strategic goals and I received a very clear answer: growth of research measured by the number of publications (in good scientific journals) as well as increase of income from students' fees, especially from graduate and postgraduate programs since they had a better margin than all other offerings. Setting priorities and allocating resources (financing infrastructure, research, scholarships etc.) in case of such goals is not complicated and requires creation of a simple portfolio matrix of the university's units, which is showed in Figure 4.1.

The simplest priorities are the maximization of financing of units in the upper right area and eliminating or starving units in the bottom left area. The strategic problems are the remaining two types of units. Units able to generate mainly research should receive resources for research and be subject to a regular control of productivity in terms of effective use of allocated resources. Units able to generate mainly money are classical 'cows' – we shouldn't finance them too much (apart from necessary infrastructure and appropriate number of lecturers), but we shouldn't starve them either. To such a proposal of priorities, the president reacted like any reasonable political leader. Namely, she explained

	Low research potential	High research potential
High financial inflows	Units able to generate mainly financial means	Units able to generate research and financial means
Low financial inflows or negative	Units unable to generate research and financial means	Units able to generate research mainly

Figure 4.1   Portfolio matrix of university's units according to their research and financial potential

that a clear formulation of such rules of allocating resources would mean a genuine revolution and would create such upheaval and conflicts at the university that it was not even worth trying it. Taking into account the specificity of such an organization as a university, she was certainly right.

From this point of view, the business world is simpler than the world of nonprofit institutions. All true business leaders I have consulted or researched in emerging markets of Central Europe are able to define priorities and are very categorical in doing so.[18] The priority of their actions in the 1990s was to regularly experiment. It was a reasonable way of looking for opportunities in the emerging and changing market, on which an analytical set up of long-term investment projects was fairly pointless. All good entrepreneurial companies were ready to fight, innovate and dominate. Their founders indicated the general strategic domain by choosing industry and products. They determined clear goals of growth, and one of the typical priorities was broadly understood to be innovation and experimentation, which managers were permitted to carry out, often encouraging them with incentives in form of material or symbolic prizes. For instance, the company SMG/KRC (market research leader in Poland in the 1990s, acquired by Millward Brown in 2000) undertook within its life cycle attempts to do all possible types of research – from political to marketing, awarding a prize for innovative approach toward research (for example, a special medal Virtuti Researcheri, a lunch prepared by the CEO, a one-month bonus added to the regular pay). Kamis, after dominating the market of herbs and spices (over 40% of Polish market), successfully experimented with mustards, a cheap GALEO brand and food concentrates. AMBRA, a leading sparkling wine producer in Central Europe, constantly experimented with products, launching new brands of wine, vermouth and vodkas (e.g. Wild Rose for women). Most of these experiments in production and marketing turned out to be a limited success or a plain failure. In each of these cases, company leaders were unequivocal in their decisions and treated failure as an important experience to learn from and ordered projects to be shut down immediately, regardless of the already incurred costs.

Summing up, priorities are a derivative and a complementation of the strategic goal. They determine what precisely should be done in a given period (what initiatives to launch) in order to achieve goals. There can be just a few priorities, because no organization is able to truly implement many priorities at the same time. Simply put, none of them has enough resources and potential to coordinate that many actions. A practical rule is three to five (in case of a big company!) priorities in a given period. These priorities, and only they should – according to the rule of Pareto – receive most organizational resources: attention of leaders, higher financing and material resources as well as the best people.

Company business model – a rule of an envelope

Apparently, the story goes, some time ago a young researcher appeared at Edison's lab with an ingenious idea. He claimed that he had discovered a formula of a super solvent, which could dissolve absolutely anything. Edison listened to the idea carefully and asked just one question: 'all right, so in what packaging are you going to keep it?'

While developing strategy, we deal with a similar problem. Let's assume that leaders have a certain cognitive map, which makes sense and generally reflects properly the company's environment. Based on this, they determine organizational boundaries with their decisions concerning markets, products and distribution technologies. They also formulate limited number of goals and priorities for action. The question arises how to take these decisions in a sustainable way and how to make them operationally feasible. The role of packaging, which in a normal company keeps the three elements of strategy together, is played by this business model. I call it the rule of the envelope, in order to highlight two aspects of the business model.

First, it is like an envelope into which you put particular interrelated decisions. Second, an envelope is not a box into which you can put many things. An envelope has limits. If you put too much into it, it will tear and everything will fall out. That is why there should only be three related elements in it: resources, capabilities and a configuration of their combinations. In such a way, the business model gives answer to three questions linked to the need of achieving complex strategic goals:

– What resources does the company need on a given territory?
– What capabilities are needed?
– In what way resources and competences should be configured, that is, what will the value chain look like?

Since theoretically and practically one can imagine many choices within each of these areas, it gives companies a huge opportunity to develop a variety of strategic choices and ways of implementation. Relatively few of these recipes for action will be extremely effective, but many will be acceptable, feasible and financially reasonable.

Strategic resources

The substances every business model is built of are resources and strategic capabilities. Resources are what the organization has and/or controls. Typical examples are buildings, location, machines, technology, brands, patents and employees. They are necessary to conduct any organizational activity. The majority of resources are bought and sold on the market, they have their price, and information concerning their location is fairly available. Some resources, especially intangible ones, have special properties – it is difficult to acquire and sell them on the market and to imitate or replace them. Classic examples of such resources are know-how of employees, loyalty of customers, company reputation and accumulated knowledge. That is why, in theory, these resources are called strategic assets.[19]

The logic of asset control is similar on an economic and a company level – you need to have property rights and effectively protect and use them. Classical resources of each company are quite similar and most often can be seen in the company's balance sheet. Buildings and equipment are subject to free commerce and that is why they are easily imitable or replaceable. A more complex situation appears in case of assets such as locations and technologies. Spaces with intensive traffic occupied by new petrol stations in Warsaw, Chicago or Guangzhou are a resource, which actually isn't subject to commerce. This is why in many crossings in the world, each corner is occupied by a petrol station of a different global company. Technologies are protected by patents, and if the company owning them decides not to license them, the only possibility for competitors is to find a substitute in the form of a new technology. Sometimes strategic assets are not so evident. Good examples are pipelines and railroads whose great importance consists, among other things, of the fact that they give the owner an opportunity to use the right of the road and to lay fiber optics highways along the pipeline or the rails. Together with growth of global markets and tougher competition, ever more often and on many territories, the keys to success are intangible resources such as company reputation, product brands and social capital – norms, values, knowledge and motivation of employees.

Reputation increases the recognition of the company, attracts the best employees, increases the bargaining power vis-à-vis suppliers and customers, stabilizes operations of the company in conditions of seasonality, economic cycles and crises.[20] Brands allow the company to impose higher prices than competitors, quickly introduce new products as an extension of existing products, create new markets by transferring the brand onto new products, like Harley-Davidson or Ferrari do by letting their brands to perfumes, Caterpillar to shoes and Cartier to luxury products – from watches to fountain pens to ties and lighters.

The increase of the importance of intangible resources as strategic assets is not followed very much by the logics of our financial reports. The balance sheet is supposed to reflect company property. But today's balance sheet model, which was born in the 19th century, was reasonable when companies' profits soared when the bigger and the heavier their products were. The key role was played by material assets. In order to earn an additional million in sales, an average company needed to invest at least 15,000–200,000 euros in working capital, that is, liabilities and reserves. Additionally, they needed to regularly finance investments – equipment, means of transport, warehouses – in order to balance their depreciation. In the new economy, it all stops being so evident. Enterprises acting according to the *just-in-time* rule or hypermarkets financing their operations with debt have a negative working capital. Thanks to improvements of the production organization, normal enterprises need many fewer physical assets in order to achieve increase in production than they used to ten or twenty years ago. Finally, an essential role is attributed to the invisible intellectual capital – people, results of research, brands, customer and employee loyalty. In some industries (software, telecommunications, pharmaceuticals, consulting and education etc.), this capital is so important that finance experts try to somehow determine their value.

Let's look for a moment at the reasoning of Baruch Levy, an accounting professor, and assume that we have a company with a roughly 15 million dollars income. Looking at its balance sheet, we see that it has around 50 million in financial assets and 100 million in material assets. An average income on financial assets expected after tax equals about 5 percent, so financial assets equal 2.5 million dollars of income. An average expected income on material assets equals 7 percent, which explains additional 7 million dollars. As a result, there is an income of 5.5 million dollars, which comes from neither financial nor material assets. Levy calls it a 'residual income from intellectual capital'.[21] Dividing this income by the discount rate appropriate for the intellectual capital, you can try to determine the value of knowledge in the company! The entire process is complex and subjective, because its rates are neither historically tested, nor does it consider market objective discount rates for intellectual capital. Arguments of prominent economists and theorists of organization claiming that an enterprise actually equals accumulated knowledge, find in such a way an unexpected ally among experts in finance and accountants. The thesis that there is a passage from creating and appropriating value based on material assets exclusively toward the increasing importance of immaterial assets in this process stopped being a heresy. There is however a problem of how to create and use immaterial resources and how to use accumulated knowledge to realize strategy.

Strategic capabilities

Using strategic assets requires dynamic capabilities or core competences, which are processes. The better the company capabilities, the more actively and intelligently it can accumulate, exploit and renew all its resources. Strategic capabilities are what organizations do best and what allows them to cope with change and challenges.[22]

Many innovative companies, who in recent years have become models imitated worldwide, have built their business models based on specific capabilities allowing use of assets in a more productive way than other companies do. This is well reflected in the example of the Spanish corporation, Inditex Group, and their flagship Zara. Their basic strategic assets in 2013 are over 1750 shops (Zara calls them the 'meeting points' of the company with customers) in over 90 countries in the world. Key capabilities of Zara are related to their stores' creation and use. The skill to locate a shop is not very complicated – in the world of fashion, a shop is either in a good location or dead. No wonder Zara locates its shops in prestigious places, such as Oxford and Regent Street in London, Madison Avenue in Chicago, Fifth Avenue and Soho in New York, Ginza, Shibuya and Omotesando in Tokyo, Orchard Road in Singapore, Paseo de Gracia and Portal de l'Angel in Barcelona, Champs Elysees and Rivoli in Paris, Piazza del Duomo in Milan, Tverskaja street in Moscow, Nevski Prospect (Marten's House) in Sankt Petersburg, Stephansplatz in Vienna, Korai street in Athens (the first ecological shop by Zara) or Galeria Mokotow and Arkadia in Warsaw. Even more interesting is the fact that Zara has its own in-house architecture studio, who design shops in such a way that they actually become an architectural event and at the same time they allow for effective marketing. It also has special studios designing decorations for their giant shopping windows, which are effectively their principal marketing tools.

Another capability is the process of fast designing of new items, for which – as the annual report of the company says – the inspiration is the 'street, music, art, but more than anything else the…shop'.[23] This simple statement hides a complex capability to constantly transfer important information concerning new fashion trends between shops around the world and design studios, as well as to translate this information into new collections, which takes place every two weeks. Zara's fast-reaction capabilities present at least three important aspects. The first one is translating information into new collections, the second their production and the third, flawless logistics of delivering goods to shops – and all this has happened in a record time.

The terms 'dynamic capabilities' or 'core competences' are important and comfortable terms, because they focus on the problem of searching for an answer to the following question: what does the company do particularly well and in an exceptionally competitive way and why (i.e. based on what resources)? It's not very difficult to answer this question if you analyze McDonald's. It is obvious that their key competences are choice of location, standardization of detailed operations, engineering of fast, repetitive top-level service and creating a nice atmosphere. It becomes more complex question in the case of network switch manufacturer, Cisco, the producer of technological transportation systems, or the French insurance company AXA. Let's pause for a moment to regard the phenomenal success of AXA.[24]

Over the last 20 years the company has lived a rapid evolution. Going from small French company Ancienne Mutuelle (number 17 on the list of insurance companies in France), it catapulted itself to eventually become one of the biggest insurance companies in the world! Their formula of success was in a way simple, and actually resulted from its immanent limitations. As a small company with limited financial slack, it couldn't grow fast either by means of merger (because in such a case a bigger partner would have swallowed it) or by means of typical acquisition (because it didn't have money) or by means of organic growth (because that takes a very long time). So it chose an unusual way – it purchased cheap, badly managed insurance companies and installed in them the rigorous and tested management model by AXA. The model in question focused on cost reduction, fast decisions, integration of procedures and computer systems, as well as concentration on a limited number of profitable products and services. Analytically speaking, you can say that AXA created three basic competences: an effective management model, an effective system of acquisitions and an efficient post-acquisition management system. When it comes to the management model, AXA has relatively quickly elaborated a management model based on clear strategic choices, concentrating on insurance and asset management. It has also built a competitive advantage based on an efficient service system. Efficiency of acquisitions consists actually in AXA's analytics being able to find underinvested, badly managed companies, correctly assess their potential for growth and take the decision to buy them fast. Finally, efficiency of integration of the purchased company is the result of the company being able to impose the verified new model for action in the overtaken companies while at the same time avoiding conflicts between organizational cultures. The example of AXA shows that in spite of the fact that core competences have various forms and can be almost typical, well-managed companies can always add new, effective dimensions.

Cisco efficiently integrates purchased companies, but usually buys companies having no more than 75 employees, out of whom 75 percent are engineers. Intel effectively uses its production capacities but it uses an unequivocal rule of allocation – most of the production capacity is 'dedicated' to products offering the highest margin. Danish manufacturer of hearing equipment, Oticon, is famous for effective project management, but their rule was also to eliminate the project when its champion resigned from participating in the team.[25] Other competences – like the allocation of resources within General Electric, control of technological melting processes at high temperatures by the German champion Heraeus, new products development by Pfizer, terminal and port management by DP World, are a composition of more complex, refined and innovative rules. Regardless of whether competences are simple or complex, you need to understand them well and use them.

Well-managed companies are able to do that. These are companies who have achieved real success by using a couple of core competences, while creating new products, introducing them to the market, building a distribution network, creating the brand or carrying out an effective acquisition. Most 'normal' companies either don't have core competences at all, or don't look for a clinical and clever answer to the question concerning their key resources and capabilities – and that is why they don't usually entirely understand their own business model.

Value chain

The last aspect of the business model is to configure company assets, processes and capabilities into a unique and understandable value chain.[26] It is the main vehicle for the strategy realization, which ensures the answer to three questions (strategic dilemmas):

1. What activities and actions are key for the financial success of the company?
2. What basic opportunities and limitations in the company's growth are created by the given value chain?

3. To what degree is the given configuration of the value chain resistant to attacks of competitors through imitation, substitution or innovation?

In various periods, questions concerning key activities, potential limitations and the uniqueness of the given value chain enjoyed different 'best' answers. But all three have always been important, because the right answer to the question decides about the company's effectiveness today and in the future. The period when a typical value chain was dominating was determined by the time when all three answers were mutually complementary, or in other words the given value chain simultaneously allowed for control, growth and protection against competitors' attack. Changes in the logics of industry operations (e.g. consolidation processes, new legal regulations), technological breakthroughs (technology change, new standards and Internet) and aggressive competitors have unavoidably provoked a new situation, where any financial formula, any set of assets and capabilities and any given value chain linking them together have met limitations or elements of its configuration has become mutually conflicting. Therefore, winning business models constantly evolve, and the rules of value chain design continue to evolve. In other words rules linking resources, people and costs evolve. In an organization, they play a role of the DNA code and that is why various rules generate different 'kinds' of value chains, from which three are the most typical: Operator's, Integrator's and Conductor's. Each of them has its own genetic strengths and weaknesses; each uses and generates different resources and key competences, each works a little differently on different territories.

Operator's model

The Operator's Model means a focus on a selected aspect of the value chain: creation of constructions and technologies (Research Operator), production (Production Operator) or sales (Marketing Operator). The genotype of an Operator is simple. The company concentrates on doing one thing well, and the company configuration is submitted to this single basic activity. A good example of a Production Operator is Portuguese company, ColepCCL. It is the biggest European contract producer of personal hygiene products, as well as cosmetics and OTC medicine. Colep started in 1965 as a manufacturer of metal packaging, and later ventured into plastic packaging. Further on, by means of consecutive acquisitions and a final merger with a British company CCL, it became large but invisible to the average customer, producer. In a hyper- or supermarket or any other kind of shop, when we reach for products made by many brand manufacturers, few customers realize that they were actually produced in ColepCCL plants across Europe.

In turn, many subsidiaries of international corporations are just Marketing Operators with a simple organizational formula, whose basis is a sales network. An army of salesmen reaches carefully selected customers. Key competence is professionalism of sales and therefore, in these companies a very important role is played by the human resources department. Its general task is to select salesmen, carefully taking into account their competences and their attitude, and then to train them regularly in a broad spectrum of capabilities – from typically technical to negotiations and communication. The better the army of salesmen is trained and motivated, the bigger the Marketing Operator's success. All other activities apart from logistics, sales and service are either secondary or conducted in some central location across the world.

The end of the 1990s brought a new version of an Operator model utilizing the Internet in order to swim in the sea of information, and therefore called a Navigator. The charm of the Navigator business model consists in the fact that material assets are limited, because the domain is the net and the essence of activity is helping in getting access to useful information. Examples of Navigators are Internet web sites such as Google, Yahoo, Baidu, Yandex or Facebook, but also Internet companies such as Amazon, Alibaba or eBay. At the end of the 1990s they created a new value using the fact that Internet gave birth to a specific type of market.[27]

First, it is a market of creating, manipulating and using new substance composed of information. Second, it is a market composed almost exclusively of fragments of an entity – there are no integrated chains, no ready products or services. Each piece of information is, by definition, incomplete, which is why each customer has to create from the existing excess of substance a precise, necessary product that he or she needs. Third, it is a market of an endless number of suppliers and customers. Everyone can create his or her own web page and load it with information, work out links to other pages and try to be closer to pages with more visits. All this would lead to a market of total excess and limited chaos, where for a normal person, the time and cost of reaching any relatively 'entire' product previously available in a specialized, dedicated book (e.g. information on battles of Greek gods or types of the organizational structure) would be too high. Thus, a new type of company naturally emerged – Internet navigators. Their aim is to help users to find their way in the net and to diminish the complexity of the process of searching for information. At the end of the 1990s, Navigators seemed to be a completely new, almost futuristic business model, about whom there have been books written, case studies and countless articles in the business press. Stock exchanges around the world were estimating the potential of their future income to be very high through stock exchange capitalization equaling hundreds of billions of Euro. But at the turn of the twenty-first century, these hopes were adjusted, as was the stock value of these firms. There were two reasons for that.

The first one is the logic of the Internet as a terribly competitive market with low entry or exit barriers, and customers are not keen to pay for subscription services of any company, since one can usually have it for free from other navigators. The second problem of Navigators consists in the fact that the limited competitive advantage and resources (mainly technology and access to customers) are based on a weak organizational basis, because they control just a minimum fragment of the value chain. That is why only the best Navigators have such a strong market position like Baidu, Alibaba, Amazon, Facebook or Google.

The power of the business model of Goggle fascinates observers, because of the inseparably linked strategy and IT technology.[28] The point of departure of Google's strategy is the mission of digitalization, organization and mass availability of information resources worldwide. Key choices of the company are to focus on improving the very effective learning algorithm by searching the net (immaterial component of strategic assets), which made Google the most popular Internet search engine; to devote huge investments to technical infrastructure (material assets is a net of over million servers); and to create and manage the ecosystem of constantly cooperating suppliers of contents, suppliers of advertisements and creators of new software and applications (key strategic capability of Google). The essence of Google's business model is linking the process of searching the net and using network services with advertisements and purchases. That is why key choices, assets and capabilities constantly complement acquisitions of companies offering innovative products (Picasa, YouTube, DoubleClick, Urchin and so on), new own services (Gmail, AdWords, Maps, Google News and so on) and a net of strategic alliances.

Like Google, eBay is also a classic Navigator – it doesn't see or send material goods, it is simply a platform facilitating interaction between sellers and buyers on the Internet, and containing numerous micro markets, where these users can easily make business and create their own auctions. The company also introduced a number of innovative value-added services such as their models of auctions and the safety of transactions, thanks to credit cards, as well as a system of business references, where an 'honest' transaction garners an 'honest' rating from the buyer, thereby increasing the market chances of a given user.

However, companies like eBay, Baidu, Google, Facebook, Yandex or Amazon are a rare kind of effective Navigators. Many Internet companies trying to master this model of configuration actually have great difficulties resulting from the causes I have mentioned – limited resources and a weak architecture. One thing you can say about their future is that it will certainly be interesting and difficult.

Integrator's Model

In the 19th and 20th centuries, the fundamental business model was born. Namely this was the extended upstream and downstream model of the Operator, which it allowed for control over all important assets and capabilities, as well as the whole process of creation and appropriation of margins. In this sense, it was and still is the most perfect and the most competition-resistant business model. A classic example of implementation is the model of action executed at the beginning of the 20th century by the aforementioned Ford Corporation. They were processing iron ore from their own mines to make the steel used in the production of metal plate, as well as rubber for tires from their own plantations, whereas cars were transported with their own boats and trains to Ford's selling points. The integrated model of the company allowed H. Ford to produce the T Model on an unprecedented scale and at a low cost, whereas its share on the American market jumped from almost 0 to 55 percent. Next, the integrated value chain was successfully used in market economy and above all in planned economy, becoming a standard model of conducting business in many industries – from heavy industries (steel, chemistry and shipyards) to typical consumer goods (cosmetics, food).

The logic of the Integrator's value chain is twofold. First, it is the logic of controlling all margins and the minimization of disturbances, which allows us to understand the difference between priorities of this business model under planned economy and under market economy. In the case of a market economy, crucial importance was ascribed to the fact that through control over consecutive activities, the company could control and overtake the added value created in the area of the whole business chain: from delivery, through production, to marketing. Simply speaking – Integrator was appropriating all possible margins. In the case of a planned economy, the Integrator's priority wasn't to overtake value but to minimize uncertainty and disturbances brought on by market scarcities. That was why big socialist economic firms and conglomerates tried to create a value chain, which would be self-sufficient – much the way Ford's empire was at a certain moment of time.

The point of departure, both for overtaking margins and eliminating uncertainty is integration: backward and forward. In the first case, the company tries to control supplies, which can be done in different ways. In an extreme case, the Integrator simply overtakes control over supplies through a buyout of suppliers and an implementation of its own organizational solutions, ensuring a coherence of activities within the whole value chain. In a symmetrically similar case, the supplier became an Integrator, overtaking his customers, which was classic of mergers in the first half of the 20th century of oil and chemicals companies. Oil companies merged, then bought refineries and then reached for control over the distribution channel that is, petrol stations. Delivery and production are carefully controlled by companies based on the Integrator's Model. Research and Development is conducted in the company's laboratories, constructions and technologies of workshops are prepared by appropriate functional divisions, and all of the important detailed operations that determine the product's quality or control over technology, are conducted within the company.

The Integrator behaves in conformity with the classic transaction economics rule that a firm shouldn't outsource production of elements (or whole phases of the production process) that are complex and in which the whole specification (description of both technical and functional parameters) is not evident. However, a firm can and should outsource production of elements or operations, which are universal, simple and easy to replace or complement in case of problems. Apart from minimizing transactional costs, the Integrator's behavior is influenced by the dominant logics of autarchy. In times of planned economy, big companies in socialist countries so strived for such control over the production process that many even opted for an internal production of screws and springs.

As the Integrator effectively gains control over research and development, supply and production, it also attempts to reach for the process of distribution and sales. For such a company the latter constitutes a natural extension of the production process, because this is the place where the previously created added value can be overtaken in the form of the margin paid by the customer and where the important information concerning customers resides. That is why integrators sometimes buy their suppliers and overtake control over the sales process. The logic of an Integrator is effective as long as the keys to success are scale of production, constituting the main mechanism of cost decrease, repetitiveness of production, maximization of market share, possibility of diversification and lack of possibility to overtake the created value through the channel of final sales. All these elements are still very important in production of consumer goods. Because of this, the Integrator's Model has survived and even still thrives.

Noble Group, like its competitors, the American Cargill or the Anglo-Swiss Glencore (recently merged with Xstrata), is an example of such a business model. Noble Group specializes in management of world chains of supplies on the market for food (mainly soya, sugar and rice), metals (ores of iron, aluminum and alloys) and energy (coal, coke and ethanol). Integration in the version by Noble Group consists of both investments in suppliers and in technical and economic control of the whole chain of supplies – from suppliers to customers. The web page of the company underlines it very strongly, showing the power and the real character of the Integrator's Model: 'Since our beginnings over 20 years ago, Noble Group has grown into a global business with real production capabilities, supplying the real world with real products. We have been painstakingly building a tangible business with real ports, real warehouses and physical mines. We own origination points, we produce and process our own raw materials, and we control the supply pipeline from beginning to end.'[29] Clear strategic choices, regular enlarging of company boundaries, a clear goal of growth and an unequivocal business model led to the company's spectacular success. Since its start-up in 1987, Noble Group has risen to become Asia's largest diversified commodities trading company, one of the biggest and best integrated companies in the world (ranked number 91 in the 2012 Fortune 500).

The example of Noble Group shows that the Integrator's Model, although unfashionable in the modern times of outsourcing and innovative, short value chains, can be still very effective. However, it's not a dominant model, because in many markets, total integration slowly loses its significance. It results from several reasons. Scale of production stops being the main mechanism of global mass production, costs decrease in the world of flexible production systems, in which previous typical fixed costs are reduced or become variable. Complex computer software for all stages of production, and for supporting activities of the ERP type, allows us to link with one another and optimize the performance of production systems of suppliers and customers, additionally reducing costs and increasing speed of action. Repetitiveness and standardization of production stopped being a value in the situation where customers search for products, services and solutions adjusted to their unique needs and expectations. Deregulation of economies and increasing global competition questioned the value of the maximiza-tion of market share, when in practice it is still possible, but ever more difficult, to dictate prices and block entry on domestic markets to new competitors. Finally, the emergence (especially on the market of fast moving consumer goods) of big retail networks such as Tesco or Metro and progress of the Internet commerce moved the opportunity of con-trolling the whole value chain from producers toward customers. That is why many companies started to build a new configuration of the value chain – a Conductor.

Conductor's Model

In an organizational sense, the Conductor's Model means a company configuration, which instead of integrating, coordinating and con-trolling all activities, outsources all secondary or peripheral activities. Thanks to this it creates networks of partners acting for the benefit of the common success by means of a classic cooperation, but also through licenses, strategic alliances, joint ventures and other organi-zational forms. The result is emergence of a company similar to what Ch. Handy correctly compared to a three-leaf clover.[30]

The first leaf stands for professional employees, who thanks to their unique competences are very well paid and indispensable, but ever less numerous. The second leaf stands for specialists and subcontractors performing routine activities – starting from suppliers of complicated expertise (e.g. lawyers) or prototype elements, through service of the production process and supplies of screws or springs and ending with cleaning and protection of the plant. For instance, during a certain period, a Polish subsidiary of Citibank outsourced such tasks as adminis-tration and real estate management, as well as catering services (Sodexo), accounting (PWC), correspondence (Polish Post), data processing (EDS), telecommunication and information network maintenance (AT&T Solu-tions). Some countries, for instance Ireland, Slovenia, India and recently also Poland actually began to specialize in the role of supplier of various types of services (data recording and conversion, call centers, data anal-ysis and processing, information and expertise system service) because American and European companies decided to outsource everything apart from their key competences. Initial projections show unbelievable possibilities of growth – in India, only the information service of Con-ductors constituted a potential source of employment for 1.1 million specialists and of turnover reaching about 17 billion dollars by 2008.[31]

The third leaf represents employees hired only for a determined period of time. They are part-time employees hired to carry out precise tasks and projects, or persons employed during times of seasonal peaks (airports during summer holidays, shops during Christmas, manufacturing plants during sudden economic booms or seasonal demand, consulting companies in case of excess of orders, universities for conducting additional lectures), constituting – by choice or by force – an ever more numerous professional group. Companies evolving toward the model of a 'three-leaf clover' deconstruct – to use the jargon of consultants – their value chain. There is a whole range of specific reasons for this deconstruction: adapting concentrated strategy, getting access to competences on the best world level (e.g. in the era of information processing), diminishing risk and costs of operations, liberation of capital and its allocation to other applications, acquisition of new resources and capabilities. The new reason is technological progress, which renders customers unable to use functional possibilities of products and services fully, whereas links between particular components of the product are already standard within the industry, like in case of computers and telecommunications. In such a case, traditional product refinement, best carried out by integrated companies, doesn't lead to either increase of income, or to increase of market share. Advantage is gained only by companies concentrated on a certain fragment of the value chain capable of innovating, reacting quickly and a quasi-modular cooperating with other companies in order to realize specific, and often unique, orders.

One of the most interesting examples of a company following this path is that of large Indian conglomerate, Bharti Enterprises, operating in telecommunications, commerce, financial services and agriculture. It follows the Conductor's strategy in an atypical way – by means of 'renting' not small, but big and competent international companies, who are hired to manage various fragments of its operations. Its partners and/or subcontractors are, among others, IBM (telecommunication infrastructure management), Alcatel-Lucent (fiber-optics), del Monte (agriculture), Vodafone (mobile phone infrastructure management), Wal-Mart (retail network of the Cash & Carry type management) and AXA (insurance). This way, Bharti ensures the best level of resources and competences in the world, which it links together creating a strategy of regular growth, diversification and internationalization.

Precise rationale for deconstruction are different and they have their unique conditions, but the advantage of a company following a Conductor's Model depends on the answer to one of the most classic questions: will additional costs of coordination, resulting from taking the given activity beyond the area of direct control, be compensated by advantages from lower costs of purchasing a given subset or service from a specialized supplier? The logic of an effective deconstruction of the value chain depends mainly on two conditions: the need for a physical closeness to the phases of the transformation process and the specialization advantages.

There is no important reason for the research and development department in Nike to have to be physically close to the manufacturing plant, the *contact center* of Orange or Impel to be close to the headquarters, or the purchasing department in Dow Chemicals to be close to production in order to coordinate with it its everyday activities. In turn, there are good reasons why the quality control division taking regular samples from a chemical installation should constantly coordinate its actions with manufacturing. Similarly, there are good reasons why the human resource department in a consulting company should conduct current observation of young employees dedicated as high potentials: future leaders and partners.

A practical recommendation, which results from the needs for coordination, is as follows: the bigger the needs for coordination, the less sense it makes to deconstruct a company searching for effectiveness, because the costs of coordination are higher – even taking into account modern telecommunication, information and management systems.

The second condition of outsourcing is created by specialization advantages. The bigger they are, the higher the probability of a well-managed company opting for outsourcing or alliance to achieve them. Combining these two dimensions (coordination and specialization) we get three generic cases:

–   A case of high economies of scale and scope and low need for integration – in this case deconstruction through outsourcing and alliances and development of conductor business model creates added value,
–   A case of low economies of scale and scope and high need for integration when the model of an integrated company has a visible advantage,
–   A case of average economies and needs for integration, where the decision to pass from an Integrator's architecture to a Conductor's architecture is risky and complex, as is well shown in the changing fate of Cisco Systems in the last decade.

Cisco built an extremely effective and highly admired Conductor's configuration in the 1990s, thanks to which its leading position on the information and telecommunication equipment market seemed unthreatened. The company grew in the 1990s with the pace of over 75 percent per year, and in the year 2000, thanks to the capitalization of 550 billion dollars, it became the biggest company in the world from the capital point of view. Using Internet and Intranet, the company built a huge global network of suppliers, who were implementing current production of orders (about 80% of all company production!) in conformity with the specification delivered by Cisco. Equipment was remotely tested by Cisco's servers, and then an integrated shipment was delivered to the final customer (often not known to suppliers). Cisco acquired new technologies mainly by means of effective acquisitions, whose pace rose during 1999–2000 to two per month. However, the Conductor's configuration revealed its limitations in the situation of a drastic decrease of demand at the beginning of 2001. Because of the endlessly increasing market demand, and as a result of the need to wait several months before complex orders were fulfilled, Cisco entered into long-term contracts with suppliers. Over time, the whole network became inertial. Together with the conviction about the unlimited effectiveness of the business model, it provoked a slow reaction of Cisco vis-à-vis the decreasing demand, and that was how the domino started to collapse. Many companies from the area of *e-commerce* stopped paying, they also decreased orders or went bankrupt. Stock of parts and products increased to over 2 billion dollars and close relations with suppliers, who had made considerable investments in assets and personnel expecting an increase of orders, suddenly deteriorated because of a dramatic decrease in orders. Some acquisitions turned out to be a failure, and in other cases engineers and managers of the overtaken companies, not being able to adapt to the culture of a big company, started to look for new jobs elsewhere or created their own companies. Lack of strong integration within the value chain delayed the flow of information and the process of taking decisions. As a result, the fairy tale about a magical business model of Cisco ended.[32]

However, the company drew conclusions from this lesson, both on the level of strategic domain and business model. They diversified their domain and entered, among others, the market of server manufacturing, centers of data processing, telecommunication and wire services for individual customers, serving mass events and even production of wireless loudspeakers. Enlarging the company's boundaries provoked changes of priorities, because the company collided with previous partners, for example, IBM and HP, which suddenly noticed Cisco on their territory as a competitor instead of a traditional supplier.[33] The natural extension of the changes in domain and strategic priorities were

Cisco's investments in new products, assets and technical competences as well as an increasing integration of the value chain. All this made the company start from the beginning to solve the puzzle of its environment and new competitors, determine boundaries of its territory, define goals and priorities and build a more integrated business model. Its clear concept of a competitive advantage, the product of the previous strategy, will also have to be redefined, following actions of competitors. In April 2009 Oracle decided to purchase Sun Mircosystems, also potential acquisition target for IBM, treating it as a potential weapon against Cisco. In November 2009, Hewlett-Packard purchased 3Com, one of the leaders of the corporate computer network market. HP decided to pay shareholders a 40 percent bonus of the latest quotations of 3Com shares for two reasons. First, by purchasing 3Com it acquired a strong weapon against Cisco in the area of its key corporate products. Second, 3Com had a very strong position on the most important market – China. Over one half of its products come from there and over 300 of 500 greatest Chinese corporations and 70 percent of government agencies use the equipment of 3Com.[34]

Summary

If we look at the degree of complexity of choices and actions that a company has to take in order to implement a strategy, any executive or leader may be scared. There are simply many of them, they all entail trade-offs, and what is more, most of these choices need to be made in conditions of lack of sufficient information. That is why strategic management is not simple and easy – neither in theory, nor in practice. Passion requires discipline. And neither passion, nor discipline come from the environment – they have to be a part of the company's identity. Fortunately, no organization has to take and implement decisions concerning the area of activities, goals and business model at the same time. In case of a small, one-product company operating on the local market, most of these choices are natural and take place in an evolutionary way. For instance, the company starts to produce one product and to sell it on the local market. With time, it adds products (it widens scale and extent of activity) and broadens its area of activity (it enlarges the territory).

The biggest Chinese producer of nonalcoholic beverages, Wahaha Group, is a model example of such an evolution. The company started small, selling milk to students in schools of Hangzhou in the late 1980s. It slowly widened both the extent of products (by multivitamin beverages and mineral water) and the territory of its operations.

Purchasing bankrupt state enterprises, it increased production capacity and decreased costs of local distribution. Through alliance with Danone, it got access to modern technologies and distribution systems and built a business model. Because the strategy of Wahaha was effective, it grew rapidly, which provoked new challenges – how to further enlarge the territory, what goals to set, how to build the business model? The company grows and intelligently links its decisions with geographical markets, customers and products. For instance, the product called Future Cola was first introduced in rural areas, where price constitutes the key determinant and where at the same time it didn't have to compete with the strong position of Coca-Cola and Pepsi, operating mainly in cities. In 2003 it started internationalization by entering the US market, focusing on the West coast and Chinese local communities. In October 2009, it broke away from its alliance with Danone after a spectacular two-year conflict, which won it patriotic support in China. This means that in strategy, they decided to opt for a direct competitive confrontation with big international corporations.

The more the company grows, the more complex it becomes. For a diversified company operating on international scale, the degree of complexity and uncertainty of the process of developing and modifying strategy is high. Fortunately, it takes a long time before the company becomes a global concern, and during this time the strategy, as well as the most important effect created on the junction of passion and discipline – the competitive advantage – are clarified.

5
The Effect of Passion and Discipline – Competitive Advantage

Advantage is always local and temporary

To reiterate, strategy is the theory of organization effectiveness. In practice, it requires passion and discipline, because if we want to achieve extraordinary results, we cannot act in an ordinary way. This is the mantra of strategic management – from classical books by P. Drucker, through works of K. Ohmae, K. Andrews, M. Porter, G. Hamel, A. J. Slywotzky to the *Blue Ocean Strategy* by W. Ch. Kim and R. Mauborgne.[1] Ordinary action produces ordinary results. In strategic categories, thinking and acting means that the company is looking for a way to act differently than others, but it is a particular way. We are interested here in repetitive actions, which set the company apart from the competition (distinction) and simultaneously ensure extraordinary results – or in other words, a competitive advantage. In this sense, every competitive advantage is a temporary and local quasi-monopoly, that is, a niche or a position, which, when used appropriately, ensures company advantages. Both words used in the above description of advantage, 'temporary' and 'local', are very important.

First, a competitive advantage always has a temporary character. It can last long like the model of advantage based on the quality and tradition of the piano manufacturer Steinway & Sons. It can be relatively short-lived like the advantage of product innovation of the inlane skates (basically a 19th-century idea of ice skates on wheels) made famous by Rollerblade Inc. that was copied by many other producers. In any case it always has a time dimension. That is why managers of a company that has built a competitive advantage should reasonably assume that the period of the advantage's existence will be shorter rather than longer, and that it depends mainly on the behavior of competitors. This means that one needs to know who the real competitor of the company is and to have the passion to constantly renew the company's position as well as to fight against the natural tendency of complacency.

Second, advantage is always local, that is, it concerns a market with well-defined boundaries. That is why discipline in the process of defining company boundaries, as described in the previous chapters, is so important. Without a precise definition of company boundaries, there is neither the possibility to define customer needs, nor to understand possibilities of competitors. In a market with very widely defined boundaries, there are many competitors (both existing and potential), and customer needs are almost endlessly diversified. In such a situation, any definition of the competitive advantage will be just a PR formulation with a somewhat blurred shape, and not an expression of a disciplined strategic thinking. There is, of course, a certain paradox in this. Companies in well-defined territories having a visible competitive advantage constitute a natural target for all competitors. If their advantage is not rooted in resources and capabilities that are difficult to imitate or substitute, it will naturally erode; companies entering the market most often do not look at the average industry profitability or the fate of the weakest companies. Their point of reference and target to attack are leaders and their reputation and profit. A good strategy is indispensable but not a sufficient condition for a competitive advantage to appear.

Resource-based view on competitive advantage

From an economic perspective, competitive advantage is equal to the value added by a company. It is important here to distinguish value creation from adding value. Added value is defined, at level of a given firm, as the value that would have been lost, had this company withdrawn from the market. Therefore, the fact that many companies do create value (it means that the willingness to pay for their product is greater than the cost of producing them) does not mean that they have a competitive advantage – that is they need not generate profits. A brief example is illustrative here: imagine two companies, A and B, both producing identical product at a cost equal to zero. No matter how high the willingness to pay for their products is, neither of them adds value. This is simply because, if one of them withdraws from the market, no value is lost. However, if company A has a lower cost than company B, this difference would constitute its value added and hence competitive advantage. In this case, economy meets management, because from the point of view of the management theory only unique resources and capabilities are able to lead to a scenario where company has a competitive advantage.

From a theoretical perspective M. Porter noted that competitive advantage can have two faces: cost and differentiation.[2] Both faces can lead to a situation in which a given company adds value in the market. A cost advantage means the cost of operations is sustainably (but not eternally) lower than a competitors', as result of its location, access to less expensive production factors, modern technology, scale of operations or any number of other factors. A differentiation advantage leads to an opportunity to realize outstanding margins by means of high prices (exploiting high willingness to pay) without worrying about a negative reaction from customers. The source of such a luxurious position can be reputation and brand, innovative or unique offerings, or high cost of changing supplier by customers. However, the question remains how does it happen that companies possess competitive advantage? The dominant view has been for many years that the bases and drivers of these advantages are some specific company resources or capabilities, as already discussed in the former chapter. That is why this approach has been called resource-based view perspective. Let's analyze this view to understand what it actually brings to our understanding of the notion of competitive advantage and what limitations it faces.

The basic model, created many years ago by J. Barney and extended by other researchers, is simple and assumes relations between company resources, competitive advantage and effectiveness (Figure 5.1).[3]

From a theoretical perspective, it is an elegant, sequential model. Effectiveness of a company (measured with extraordinary results) is explained by existence of competitive advantage. Existence of advantage is, in turn, conditioned by access to tangible and intangible resources, which are at least valuable and rare. If resources are only valuable (which is indispensable to carry out business effectively) and rare, the advantage

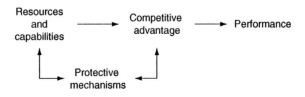

Figure 5.1   Basic model of resource-based view in strategic management

acquired by the company will be temporary, because competitors will be able to acquire such resources relatively quickly. For instance, in the 1990s one entrepreneur managing a network of restaurants in Kiev almost monopolized control over a rare resource: good cooks and waiters. Competitors reacted logically – one of them launched a school for cooks and waiters and ensured an inflow of qualified staff to the whole market. Excellent chefs are probably still rare, but for an average restaurant or pub in Kiev, a qualified cook or waiter is a valuable, yet accessible resource.

From the perspective of resource-based view, only valuable resources, rare and protected against imitation and substitution, give companies a chance to create a competitive advantage. To make this advantage sustainable and achieve an outstanding economic profitability in the long run, resources have to be complemented by specific routines to use them productively (dynamic capabilities).[4] However, there is a question: how can a company protect its resources and capabilities from imitation, substitution, obsolescence and decline?

The resource-based view states that there are two most common ways of limiting imitation and substitution. The first is to increase the specificity of the process of acquiring or developing resources by making resource effectiveness path and time dependent. Examples of such resources can be found in the historic power of the brand Steinway and the capabilities of employees of this company in the area of piano manufacturing honed for almost 150 years. Another example is the qualifications of Swiss employees in the electro-engineering industry, or the cumulated knowledge of Mexican construction material manufacturer, CEMEX, in its ability to quickly and effectively improve and integrate acquired companies.

The second key obstacle to imitation is a casual ambiguity of configuration of resources, making it difficult to understand the impact of particular resources on the process of creating advantage (the so-called causal obscurity). A classic example is the configuration of the management system in IKEA or Toyota, which have been described in world literature and reports of consultants, but which has remained so complex and nontransparent that competitors have been unable to copy it over last 20 years. Both these phenomena – the specificity of the process of developing resources and the complexity of the ways to link and exploit them – create key protective mechanisms in the theory of strategy, as well as key mechanisms to isolate the company from competition and its operations.[5]

The simplicity of this model has two very serious traps with theoretical and practical consequences. The first is the relationship between effectiveness and competitive advantage, and the second the relationship between resources and competitive advantage.

Trap 1: advantage and results

For many years, academics and managers assumed that the existence of advantage must lead to high company effectiveness, and thus also to attainment of above-average industry returns. An indirect consequence of this is the attitude toward company results that are treated as a measure (index) of the existence or nonexistence of competitive advantage. This meant that in theory, and in practice, the three-stage model (resources – advantage – results) was simplified to two elements: resources and results. As a consequence, researchers were looking for the impact of intangible resources (e.g. human capital, social capital, knowledge, reputation, experience and organizational culture) and tangible resources (e.g. location, specific assets and nonspecific assets, economies of scale and economies of scope, composition of the board of management) on company results. In this perspective above-market returns meant the possession of a competitive advantage as a result of access to valuable, rare and difficult-to-imitate or substitute resources. Consultants following this line of thought were constantly recommending companies to invest in such resources – especially intangible assets. It is a rather problematic approach because there are at least two assumptions hidden behind this – namely the relative homogeneity of competitive advantage and the automatic opportunity to capture profits resulting from its possession.

The first assumption treats the competitive advantage as relatively homogeneous entity, something almost precise, tangible, a propriety of the whole organization vis-à-vis its competitors. Even the old common SWOT technique didn't simplify reality to such a degree, because it assumed that an organization always had some strengths and weaknesses compared to its competitors. That is why in practice, the SWOT analysis led to conclusions regarding which company strengths and weaknesses should be invested more in order to either increase company advantage on the market or to decrease lack of advantage. In a similar vein, in the practice of management, a 'competitive advantage' must exist in parallel with a 'competitive disadvantage', and both will have a certain impact on the company results.[6]

The essence of differentiating competitive advantage and competitive disadvantage is to notice that they are not entirely symmetrical notions. Lack of advantage doesn't necessarily have to mean the company doesn't have valuable and rare resources in given areas like some of its competitors. The problem is that even if two companies have identical resources, one of them could be able to organize and use them better than the other, and because of this achieve an advantage. This means that the thinking that a competitive advantage is a kind of a homogeneous entity (frequently taking place in managerial practice) is most often a myth.[7] A more realistic assumption is that a company has certain advantages as well as disadvantages, and what is more, these can co-exist in one area of the company (e.g. distribution or human resource management). It is not at all obvious how or if they complement each other because it depends on the context of the company's operations.

It is a real challenge for both scientists and managers. In an ideal but trivial case (e.g. monopoly), when a company has a clear advantage and has no disadvantages, we can observe extraordinary economic results. Likewise, the case of a company with no advantage and clear disadvantages will be very simple. The normal world of organizations is more accurately represented by co-existence of advantage and disadvantage, which is to say having strengths and weaknesses at the same time. In both cases, companies can have results that differ from theoretical expectations. This is connected to another problem – the actual possibility to use the advantage to capture extraordinary results.

The model of the resource-based view presented in Figure 5.1 assumes that in a given context the company is able to capture profit resulting from its competitive advantage. The fact that a given company has some advantages, as well as clear and differentiating competences, doesn't mean that it will obtain equivalent benefits from the market. In conditions of changes and globalization, they can actually be captured by stronger players in the remaining fragments of the value chain (suppliers or buyers) or simply by other stakeholders (e.g. by the government in the form of additional taxation). A reverse situation can take place as well – the company can accidentally capture an extraordinary part of the chain's value without actually possessing any evident advantage. Existence of such opportunities simply means that a competitive advantage is a necessary, but not sufficient, condition of above-average returns.

Trap 2: resources and advantage

The second problem is hidden in another key relation of the model, namely advantage dependence upon resources. Almost immediately after Barney's article proposed the resource-based view model, critical voices appeared, indicating its static character.[8] The basic argument was that resources – technologies, people, reputation, IT, products, brands etc., are not productive per se. Productivity can be reached only as a result of their application, which, in turn, is related to application of concrete organizational routines and capabilities. Companies that do not have capabilities allowing them to use their resources effectively will not achieve a competitive advantage.

When managers think about competitive advantage, they most often look for its sources mainly in company resources. The reason is simple: resources are a concrete thing, both tangible (location, technology, production capacity and finances) and intangible (knowledge, organizational culture and reputation). We know how to name and measure them. Analysis and measurement of capabilities is much more difficult, because we deal with a dynamic, complex category. The most important processes and organizational capabilities have a systemic character, because they simultaneously include material and immaterial components (e.g. information system, data bases and methods to use them), as well as technological and social components (e.g. the CRM system and personal relations with the main customers). The effectiveness of routines and capabilities changes as an organization learns how to exploit them and improve them in formal and informal ways. Operationalization of capabilities and their measurement are both very complex, in theory and in practice. It seems that capabilities constitute a more important category than resources, which is why in recent years we have observed a relatively dynamic advance in research attempting to measure their significance in terms of achievement of competitive advantage. Recently, they have suggested measuring the level of competitive advantage with the quality of 'business processes', which seems to be a very interesting way of thinking.[9]

Analyzing the relationship between company resources and quality of key business processes, that is, dynamic capabilities that are key to the success of the company strategy, we arrive at a theoretically (and practically) elegant model of dependences: resources – dynamic capabilities – company success. The strength of this model results from the fact that dependencies become easier, and in certain competitive situations, concrete business processes (fragments of the value chain) are of key importance. For example, in consulting this would be the recruitment of employees and maintenance of relations with the main customers. In the production of elevators, this would be design of elevators and after-sales service. In the production of sports shoes, this would be design and marketing.

Summing up, in the resource-based view of competitive advantage, after a period of turbulent growth and an immense amount of research conducted, the time has come for some self-reflection. This is manifested in an increased approval of theoretical limitations of this approach, a thorough definition of researched relations, an increased precision in measurement of the main variables as well as in search for practical applications. It means a growing maturity of the concept of competitive advantage as the main way to improve company results. So far in the theory and practice of strategy, there is no better hypothesis, statement or metaphor that could compete with the abovementioned postulate. It was highlighted by T. C. Powell, who said, 'even if deductive or inductive reasoning cannot prove that competitive advantage produces superior performance, competitive advantage has itself survived competition among rival performance theories. Perhaps we need not concern ourselves much about formal logic or epistemological truth, having gained the wisdom that in an imperfect world we work with imperfect theories, and that our task as scholars is not perfection or non-contradiction, but intellectual progress'.[10] And with this dictum in mind we can discuss types of competitive advantage in practice.

Practice of competitive advantage

The opening sentence from Leo Tolstoy's famous novel *Anna Karenina* goes like this: 'All happy families are alike, each unhappy family is unhappy in its own way.' This is also true in the practice of business. All the best-managed companies are similar. All good strategies are similar, linking passion for changes with discipline of execution. All good strategies are simple and coherent. They also have 'something' – a competitive advantage, which is the essence of every effective strategy. Without an advantage, one can speak about strategy as a coherent concept of action, but it is difficult to speak about effectiveness and extraordinary results. Practitioners are rarely passionate about discussing the value created and the value appropriated, as well as the strategic resources or dynamic capabilities previously described. Their world is most often competition and customers, and not the relatively complex, although useful, theoretical categories. That is why in the practice of management, the definition of competitive advantage focuses on indicating a precise reason a company is better than its competitors, or if it is difficult to demonstrate it *explicitly*, to indicate the basis of the company's identity and sense of uniqueness. The most typical are four practical types of competitive advantage[11]:

– Natural advantage;
– Price–performance ratio that offers differentiation compared to competitors;
– Stable relations with customers based on loyalty or high cost of changing suppliers (relationships advantage);
– System of service, which creates high entry barriers.

They are not fully separable and sometimes their effect on the market can be identical, even if the basis of advantage is different. But for practitioners, the logic is different. Only the first and the last are close to one another, because they constitute different versions of the dream of each strategist – a temporary monopoly.

Natural advantage

Over a period of years, certain companies stopped having to make visible strategic choices, because they had three natural sources of competitive advantage: location, access to resources and legal regulation. For many years and for many companies, the most typical advantage has been location. Because of the limited number of customers and high costs of transport, a local supplier of cattle, soap, jam, arms, shoes, windows or bank services could easily avoid competition, and even earn reputation and customer loyalty.

It is difficult to enter the dairy market, say, in north-east Lithuania, for any dairy from Germany, because of high costs of transport, limited purchasing power of inhabitants and readiness of local dairies to start a price war. Also, local companies have the added benefit of being able to create another facet of this advantage by playing on the local character of the company, which can in turn awaken local customer patriotism. The famous marketing campaign by Polish champion of construction supplies, Atlas, 'I love Poland', and its commercials presenting Polish knights and Teutonic knights made reference to exactly such a local patriotism and were simply saying: 'Support Polish companies.' It is a message that is effective only in a particular domestic market and in the short run, but then again, every advantage is temporary. However, highlighting the local character of the company is regularly used throughout the whole world as an important advantage of companies defining their national or regional identity. Local patriotism was present in the US when American concerns were defending themselves against the invasion of Japanese car manufacturers, and today it is popular in China as a recipe for maintaining a high pace of economic growth.

Another good example of location advantage is market size. In the 20th century, American companies always had the great natural advantage of the largest homogeneous market – one with a shared language, common currency and similar legal regulations. It allowed them to achieve a scale of activity (and cost structure) with which not many companies in Europe could actually compete. Today it is the advantage of Chinese and Indian companies. The scale of these markets, in spite of their limited homogeneity, allows companies to develop relatively quickly, whereas in Europe growth would take many years. For instance, in the Guangdong region in southern China, until recently there were over 8000 manufacturers of shoes, out of whom almost all started at the turn of the 1980s and 1990s! The latest crisis thinned their numbers, but the remaining factories still manufacture over one-third of the shoes produced worldwide. A certain part of them fulfills orders of European and American producers, but the biggest manufacturers from this region concentrate on the Chinese market, because this is where they see the biggest opportunity for growth. In 1991, Deng Yao, which already had some experience in production and distribution of shoes in the 1980s, founded a company called Belle International. In 2009 it had a turnover of over 2.5 billion dollars and controls more than 20 percent of the market of women's shoes in China (brands such as Belle, Staccato, Teenmix, JipiJapa and Tata). Daphne International, which started at the same time, has a turnover of approximately 1 billion dollars and Foshan Saturday Shoes, which started production in 1996, had 100 million dollars USD in turnover in 2009. For local manufacturers, the scale of the Chinese market constitutes an immense natural advantage and allows them to grow quickly. Another natural step for these companies is setting up operations in other Asian countries, and after reaching the scale of several billion dollars, also internationalization by venturing into developed markets.

Another typical source of advantage often connected to location is access to resources. Huguenots that were watch manufacturers and moved to Switzerland after being chased away from France at the end of 17th century got access to a qualified and disciplined workforce (especially in Geneva), which permitted them to develop production quickly. In the 1970s, OPEC countries could create a cartel dictating prices, because the demand for oil was much bigger than the supply, and the OPEC countries controlled the sources of oil. Speaking seriously, it is worth remembering that many world corporations could grow to their current position thanks at least partially to their historical advantages regarding access to resources. In the 19th and 20th centuries, for many European companies, these natural advantages were overseas colonies and the governmental protection they were enjoying there. Exploiting access to resources in Asia and Africa and by carrying out trade in a wide extent, they accumulated capital and capabilities, building genuine business empires. American companies took advantage of the same privileges in South America and the Caribbean, whereby warships and marines sent by the American government strengthened the natural advantage of these companies over local competitors and allowed them to acquire resources and build the scale of their operations.

The third natural source of monopolistic advantages are legal regulations, which are traditionally represented by all old state monopolies – from salt to spirit. Today such monopolies are rare, but they have been replaced by temporary monopolies in form of patents and trademarks. Thanks to their patents, companies such as Nobel, Xerox, Siemens, Philips, GE, Alfa Laval, Tetra Pak, IBM, Merck & Co., Pfizer or ABB control some technological processes or product characteristics in the whole world until today. Legal systems regarding protection of intellectual property, which for many companies (mainly from developed countries) has become the basis of advantage, are also one of the important problems companies in world markets deal with today. Namely, there is a range of companies practicing the strategy of 'aggressively' patenting products and process innovations, a mass registration of trademarks, as well as booking Internet domains. The advantage of firms that pursue such an aggressive strategy is that they can take quick action in the legal system and explore its imperfections. Thanks to this, they effectively force other companies to pay a 'ransom' for the right to enter a given market, to use their own brand or a given technology.

Advantage of price–performance ratio

In theory, we speak about a cost advantage and a differentiation advantage; in practice, advantage is built based on the perception of the relation between the price and the performance (quality). We can differentiate the two simplest, most extreme cases:

- A cost-price advantage for an offer of the minimum level of acceptable quality;
- An advantage based on the visible differentiation and a high level of prices.

For many years, costs have been the source of main advantage for economists, but it was only the concept of an experience curve, developed by Boston Consulting Group, that delivered operational sense to the evident truth that lower costs are better than higher costs. The term 'experience curve' was created to complement the phenomenon of 'learning curve', which had been known for many years. It was known for a long time that the effort needed to carry out routine activities decreases with time as a result of employees learning how to carry out detailed operations quicker and with more respect for technological requirements. The phenomenon of learning decreased costs because the result was a higher productivity within the same unit of time. The merit of research conducted by the Boston Consulting Group was that it indicated additional explanations for the conditions of cost reduction, apart from costs of direct workforce, and especially indicated the importance of the volume of production, as well as of specialization and the level of investments connected with it.[12] A larger scale of production – of lettuce, beer, cars or megawatts – provokes a general decrease in both fixed costs (i.e. research and development, marketing and management) for a unit of production and also variable costs. Cost decreases justify further investments, scale increase and production capacity usage maximization, which results in a further decrease of costs.

However, the experience curve had a fundamental limitation – it allowed the development of a cost strategy and the analysis of cost dynamics only for a given product assuming an unchanged production technology. The 1970s were years of seeking new perspectives of sources of cost reduction, especially facing the oil crisis and the increase of prices of raw materials. The company McKinsey became a pioneer in developing simple models of 'business systems', which in today's jargon are called 'value chains'. Later, the technique was complemented by ABC (Activity Based Costing) type accounting, which allowed understanding of the dynamics of costs of each activity, separate products, business units and common activities in diversified companies (e.g. human resource management or knowledge management). As understanding of the logic regarding activity cost creation grows, it is possible to search for sources of cost reduction – both on a company level by manipulating these elements and constantly comparing them with cost levels of competitors' particular activities as well as on the level of concrete activities. Only systematic cost control ensures effectiveness of operations, organizational efficiency and maintenance of a Spartan culture of operations that, for example, characterize Bimbo, the world's emerging multinational and largest bread baker. This Mexican company mastered execution excellence because it deals with relatively cheap perishable product, that has to be produced and delivered to thousands of points of sale worldwide, at the right time with minimum costs and waste.

Regardless of its sources, cost advantage has two particular features. First, it is economically the most fundamental competitive advantage, because it gives the company freedom of strategic choices competitors don't have. Second, in practice, only one company can have the lowest costs at a given level of quality. That is why companies which don't have a chance for cost advantage search for other possibilities and find them in differentiation and market niches.

Even if it is difficult to believe it today, at the beginning of the 20th century, one of the pioneers seeking advantage specifically in terms of product quality and differentiation was General Motors. When Alfred Sloan took control of the company, it was composed of eight main divisions producing cars customers didn't want to buy. The company was almost bankrupt. Its main competitor, Ford, was dominating the market with one, famous model – the black Ford T. General Motors couldn't effectively compete on a cost basis with an integrated company such as Ford, and that was why it created a truly innovative strategy. It liquidated the basis of Ford's success by dividing the market into five main segments.[13] Many years passed before the Sloan's innovative marketing concept, one that shaped the strategy of GM for over half a century, became a common pattern of thinking. It was gaining ground with difficulty, because the dominant philosophy of thinking was to treat most markets as markets of commodities, or in other words, an exchange of products with similar properties. After ultimately taking off, this became the new practice for marketing strategies, turning some producers into symbols representing a certain quality dimension for competitors, and moreover, for customers: Coca-Cola and Red Bull in beverages; Rolls-Royce, Mercedes, BMW or Ferrari in cars; Vestas in air turbines; Patek-Philippe, Omega and Rolex in watches; Dior, Prada, Gucci and Armani in clothes; Castellini in dental units; Tabasco in pepper sauces; Zodiac in rubber boats; Klais in organs; and Wharton, Harvard or INSEAD on the business schools front. Together with the growth of market competitiveness, companies most often create a couple of differentiation dimensions, which give their offer an unusual character.

Linking differentiating features is most important for success. There are cars certainly technically better and more interesting from a design point of view and less expensive than Honda. Not many producers are however able to link these features in a way to build the feeling of an honest offer among customers like Honda does. That is why some models of Honda (for example, Accord) were the most popular cars in many world markets for many years. The ultimate goal of differentiation is to create a company brand or a product brand and to link them to the customer (at best – for good), which makes us come closer to the third type of advantage anchored in the service system.

Relationships advantage

Natural advantage and relational advantage (price versus performance ratio) assume the existence of a limited relationship between the supplier and the customer. A large intermediary is the anonymous market and bridges are, at best, the company's reputation, product brand, and distribution and promotion systems. The relationships advantage, build on an intimate service system, assumes constant cooperation, that is, close and direct relationship between the supplier and the customer. The process of building such a relationship has three aspects.

The first is a careful selection of customers, because service means investment, and only a long-term relationship guarantees a reasonable return from such an investment. At the same time, stability of such a relationship must be valuable for the customer. Another aspect is to offer a combination of products and services, which constitute a solution for an important problem of the given customer. That is why companies carefully adjust their offers for important customer segments, trying to understand the dynamics of their needs and systematically following the level of satisfaction from service. The third aspect is the fact that companies using such a strategy often go beyond the role of a passive supplier and take partial responsibility for the effects of applying products or services, offer consulting, constantly examine customer needs and try to surprise the customer with top-quality service. Since in many markets, as a result of product and price quality standardization, the advantage of service systems starts to play a key role, it is no surprise that it attracts the attention of theorists and consultants. This results in descriptions and analyses conducted mainly based on case studies that aim to identify the most important organizational and economic conditions of the relationship development process that produces loyalty, trust and high switching costs for customers.[14]

One company where I worked as a consultant was building its relationship with customers in the following way. The company was selling advertising opportunities in a specific medium, and it specialized in a narrow group of potential buyers of advertising time and location. The company didn't hire typical salespersons to sell the product to potential buyers. People in charge of customers were called 'consultants', and that was exactly how their role was perceived. The task of each consultant was to discuss with the customer his or her needs and to check whether the selected medium was the best from the point of view of advertising effectiveness. If, based on research and discussion with the customer, the consultant drew the conclusion that the customer should use another medium, his or her duty was to tip off the customer to this information and to put the customer in contact with an appropriate company – even if it was a competitor! Research showed that effect of this strategy was exactly what was expected: customers assessed the level of service extremely high, agreed for relatively high prices and were very loyal.

Effective building of a service system advantage requires fulfillment of three rigorous conditions. The first condition is a deep knowledge of reality and customer needs through maintaining constant contact, systematic conduct of quantitative and qualitative marketing research, analyses of problems customers face in order to achieve goals and meeting expectations. The second condition is creation of a broad product and service offer well adjusted to the needs of particular segments. It is not about today's fashionable slogan claiming to offer customization, which is very difficult and expensive. It is rather about an innovative market segmentation based on well-defined expectations and needs, as for example, the American Exxon Mobil did in the second half of the 1990s.[15]

At the beginning, based on research, they identified three basic customer expectations regarding a petrol station: comfort (easy to find and get in), price of fuel and additional services (opportunity to do some basic shopping). Then they determined the hierarchy of needs of various customer groups and linking together customers with similar hierarchies of needs, created five basic segments: Road warriors, True blues, Generation F3, Homebodies and Price shoppers.

In their next move, they built careful demographic, psychographic and behavioral profiles of each of the differentiated segments. Exxon

Mobil 'discovered' that *Road warriors* earned over 75,000 dollars, traveled over long distances, ate behind the wheel and preferred full service at petrol stations. *True blues* earned less money, preferred self-service and treated a petrol station as a place to take fuel, not to buy anything else. *Generation F3* meant fuel, food, fast – they appreciated comfort, full service and the chance to complement supplies fast. Exxon Mobil focused on these three segments, because they constituted the majority of the market, and built on its stations a service system from the point of view of customer expectations and needs. The main elements of the new service system were increased number of fuel pumps, restoring pumps with full service, introducing cards allowing for a faster service (*speedpass*) and much better-stocked shops.

The third condition of development of powerful service system is to build high switching costs (economic and, if possible, also legal) for customers. Everyone can take his or her car and go to another petrol station or buy things in another supermarket, but it is much more expensive to replace a computer system, bank, telephone operator or a dominant aircraft used by airlines. In many markets companies perform a ritual dance, in which suppliers find various ways to increase the cost of changing suppliers to their most precious customers, and these customers try to lower them in order to become independent from the supplier. A traditional way to make the customer depend on supplies is through long-term contracts, but most often the benefits for the customer are lower prices and better conditions of delivery. Another way to make a customer dependent are various loyalty programs, which take a form of either lowering the price as the purchase grows, or of increasing the offer's scope for the same price. Another possibility is to systematically build and offer new valuable services, for example, additional information, database creation and processing, such as in relations of pharmaceutical companies with distributors of medicine, and the latter, in turn, with pharmacies.

A variant of this is a systematic development of a complementary offer addressed to customers, which is aimed at becoming a 'system supplier'. For example, all big companies producing industrial goods – from GE to ABB – offered their main customers a full service offer in the 1990s, that is, they proposed to overtake the planning, repair and maintenance of all machinery (regardless of who has produced them) as an element of a system offer. An advantage built on the service system means investments for both parties. The supplier invests in getting to know the customer and adjusting the service system; the customer's investment consists in the fact that the approval of a given service system decreases elasticity of his or her future choices. In an extreme version, the service system advantage starts to become – by blocking entry to competitors – the last variant of advantage, that is, creation and control of standards.

Building entry barriers advantage

Building entry barriers is obviously a modern version of the first type of advantage – the natural advantage. In the past, location and access to resources or patents were a strategy aimed at blocking access to the market and building a monopolistic position. Today, the strategy with the same goal is building entry barriers and defining standards. This version is always the effect of combination of many conditions, coincidences and conscious strategies, but some mechanisms are common; that is why, in practice, this kind of advantage appears in two forms.

The first is a quasi-monopoly of a limited market thanks to combination of tradition, technology, brand power and specific relations with customers. Some good examples are German and Scandinavian companies, which have dominated the various world market niches, such as Staedtler and Faber-Castell's for pencils, Hauni for machines for the quick rolling of cigarettes, Winterhalter-Gastronom for hotel dishwashers, Grohmann Engineering for assembly robots for microelectronic devices, Vestas for air turbines and Oticon for hearing aid devices.[16] The limited size of these markets, combined with control over technology and high importance of mutual trust between suppliers and customers creates enormous difficulties for potential competitors entering the market.

The second case is creating and controlling a standard, like in case of the distance between rail tracks, the VHS technology on the video market and the Blue-ray on the DVD market, or the most famous example – Microsoft and the Windows software. Microsoft's long dominance isn't exactly due to the quality of products themselves, but rather due to the development of a network of related companies – from Intel to computer producers and software producers who base their products on the Windows operating system. That is why, in theory, we often say that such advantages are based on the effect of a network complementarity, meaning mutual support and complementation by networks of companies, who operate like a convoy – the main company is surrounded by a group of companies called complementators.[17] An important result of network operations is the decrease of costs and risks of partners' operations as a result of creating mutual trust. In its simplest version, trust decreases costs, because instead of a thorough calculation of expenditures and profits, it allows participants to use simple decision rules, such as *tit for tat*, we work together on marginal markets in order to dominate them, and we compete on the central market, we fight together against the bigger, but separately against the smaller and so on. A network allows also for a much richer communication between participants and for a common problem solving platform on the level of entity, and not on the level of an individual company.

Wal-Mart, building a network of its suppliers, has led to a partial integration of computer systems and created opportunities of a mutual 'insight' to each other's databases. Thanks to an Internet platform, Apple has created an enormous open network of suppliers of software compatible with its iPhone, which in a short time resulted in over 500,000 applications created around the world. Alliances among good business schools, which we witness today, serve to build common course materials and joint programs, solve the problem of staff deficits thanks to the possibility of rotating lecturers between campuses, increase the quantity of resources available for students, thanks to which they increase competitiveness of all members of the network. Finally, benchmarking and knowledge transfer within the network is simpler and less expensive than through market transactions. Many years ago it started on a big scale due to General Electric, which created the Best Practices Group, that is, a group of several world companies who agreed upon a way of exchanging management experience and practices. At present, such an exchange of knowledge is the norm and members of networks rich in knowledge and information benefit from it quickly and greatly; those who remain outside the network lose distance in a way impossible to catch up, regardless of investments. Microsoft's economy and advantage were growing in its network together with creation of ever more numerous programs treating Windows as the basic environment. Usage of these programs was becoming ever more common as the importance of the Windows standard was growing. In such a way, a positive feedback was created, which led to Microsoft's domination on the market of software, Intel's domination on the market of microprocessors, Visa's and MasterCard's domination on the market of credit cards, Nintendo's, Microsoft's and Sony's on the market of games or SAP's on the market of industrial software.

The example of creating and controlling the standard by Microsoft is instructive indeed and it is very interesting for strategists and specialists in the area of law protecting competition. Two things deserve a particular attention. First, it is foolish to blame Microsoft, in spite of the fact that some of its practices were wrong and persecuted by courts and legal institutions both in the US and EC. As a company, it just made what every strategist dreams about – it almost monopolized the world market with a product of an average to good quality. Second, and more importantly, Microsoft is in the same degree the author and the 'victim' of its strategy. From the moment DOS operating system became common standard, it was worth it for all software suppliers to write 'for DOS', making it a standard and strengthening the motivation to create software compatible with DOS. For users who learned how to use the program, on one hand it meant intellectual as well as time investment, and on the other hand, high costs of a potential system change. The same holds true for the Windows environment. Microsoft only created the basis of the positive feedback's loop, in which many participants cooperated, but it didn't control the process it had launched. It only tried to strengthen it intelligently and at any cost. That is why what happened was easily predictable. It dominated the market, but antagonized everyone – suppliers, customers, employees and government regulative agencies. This is the natural fate of a company controlling the standard and therefore trying to appropriate the maximum value share created by all players participating in the game.

As a source of advantage, natural conditions constitute the oldest, simple, but very stable sources of advantage. You almost don't need to renew or improve them. Product advantages – cost and differentiation – mean constant fighting, tension and the need for a systematic run forward. That is why if there are only appropriate conditions, an optimal variant is to pass to the level of creating complex solutions, which link customers more strongly and decrease the need for constant improvement. Finally, the strategy of building entry barriers is an attempt to go back to the logic of natural conditions, a search for the way to block competitors' operations. Its success inevitably always also becomes the source of its failure. In a company controlling the standard, it provokes arrogance, in customers, aggression, and what is more, it unifies efforts of competitors. In such a way even an advantage, which seemed to be so stable and sure, becomes temporary. That is why the *dictum* nothing is eternal is right, because it describes well the practical world of competitive advantage. It is rather an exception from the rules of the game, a market deformation, which requires stable investments in new resources and capabilities. As the logic of advantage changes, one needs to change or create the company strategy once again.

What should be included in the company strategy statement?

At least once a year, CEOs of smaller or bigger companies ask me the same question: what should be included in the company strategy? And the answer isn't so simple. It is difficult to answer this question in three sentences, because the true formulation of strategy means many important decisions and resolutions. At the same time, it is obvious that managers would like to receive a simple answer, not a long lecture. What is more, since capacity of human short-term memory is limited to $7 +/- 2$ variables, it would be best if the strategy had, at the maximum, five to seven elements (and the same number of slides!), because then there is a chance that everyone will remember it. For the benefit of management practice, one can succinctly and unequivocally say what a strategy's formulation should include, but one needs to remember two limitations.

First, there is no single recipe for all companies. Elements of strategy taken into account by Gazprom, General Electric, Danone or P&G can be different from elements of strategy important for Haier, Chuba Chups, Barco, Montupet or OMV. The scale and degree of the complexity of operations will have an impact on the strategy's presentation. Second, it is worth to remember that in such a formulation, we make an enormous shortcut as we omit the whole process of gathering data about the environment, customers, competitors, as well as the diagnosis of company resources and capabilities that constitute the material for analysis and decisions indispensable in each strategy. Having in mind these two warnings, one can assume that the formal strategy formulation should include at least three, and optimally five, complementary elements. Three most important are the elements already discussed: territory of activities (strategic domain); strategic goal and type of competitive advantage.

The goal defines where we are going and it constitutes an organizational compass. One can and should complement it with a vision formulation (what the future should be), as well as a mission formulation (what the sense of our existence is), but it is strategic goal that is the key element of strategy. The territory shows where the company will operate – its definition of whom it will or will not serve, as well as products and technologies linking the market with the product. The definition of an advantage combines these two elements, because it shows which methods should be used to achieve the goal on a given territory. What, where and how – these three questions should be answered in the basic version of the strategy. In the more advanced version, it is reasonable to complement this basic statement with two additional elements: the company orientation and the source of advantage. The first is an additional clamp between the goal and the territory; the second between the advantage and the logic of the company's business model.

Company orientation

Every company strategy has a hidden internal key choice of market orientation – either the company wants to fight against precise competitors or it wants to fight for a precise segment of customers. That is why while formulating strategy it is worth taking into account a clear definition of what the company wants.

A company may choose one of two basic orientations: a confrontation with competitors or a focus on customers. Obviously, in practice strategy often has to realize both of them, but one of them is primary and the other one secondary in a given place and at a given moment of time.

The first possible orientation is confrontation with competition. The blade of the strategy is addressed against competition. The company wants to weaken or destroy precise competitors and, in such a way, strengthen its own position and its own advantage. Such has been for many years the strategic orientation of the steel conglomerate ArcelorMittal, which was consistently building its position of being the world leader through consecutive acquisitions, eliminating one rival after another. The term 'elimination' is politically incorrect, thus it is safer to use the term 'consolidation' instead, though the sense remains similar. When one reads the list of selected acquisitions of this conglomerate conducted between 1989 and 2008 (Iron & Stel Company of Trinidad & Tobago, Sibalas, Sidbec-Dosco, Hamburger Stahlwerke, Walzdraht Hochfeld GmbH, Stahlwerk Ruhrort, Inland Steel Company, Inmetal, ALFASID, Sidel, Nowa Huta, Polskie Huty Stali, BH Steel, Balkan Steel, International Steel Group, Kryvorizhstal, Arcelor, Sicarstsa, NSD, OFZ, China Oriental Group Company, M. T. Majdalani, Essen Wagner, Unicon, Laminadora Costarricense, Trefileria Colima, Gonvarri Brasil etc.), one thinks of the scene in which the heroes of the old cult film *Highlander* kept repeating: 'There can be only one.' Such is the sense of competing in mature or declining industries – it is about the fact that there can be only one at the end.

Fortunately, in this world, there are still institutions protecting consumers as well as anti-monopolistic institutions, and that is why there are normally at the endgame few players left who control the market. If the company operates in an industry subject to consolidation, the strategy should have an offensive facet – it is better to be in the consolidating group than the consolidated. Strategies of Microsoft, ArcelorMittal or Wahaha (soft drink producer in China) were above all directed against competitors. The goal of these strategies was to destroy or limit competition, and in such a way, to strengthen their own market position. It is impossible to speak in such cases about any popular, refined strategy conforming to the judo rule 'Yield, and you'll win.' A theorist will simply say that the company needs bigger resources and better capabilities in such industries and therefore has to grow through mergers and acquisitions. A practitioner will say the same but in a different way. He or she will say that only scale and strength count – simultaneous access to less expensive sources of supply and workforce, a bigger production scale and scope and an advantage in distribution and marketing.

It means a natural feedback between the choice of such an orientation and the goal and the type of competitive advantage. The goal is consolidation, and for companies that consolidate great, mass markets (chemistry, raw materials and industrial components), the basis for success is the advantage of the lowest costs. A true cost leader has to find and use all sources of cost reduction. That is why it usually will offer a standard product without any additional bonuses, and will emphasize on economy of scale and usage of an absolute cost advantage regardless of its source (inexpensive workforce, low cost of general management, low marketing expenditure, low office and rental fee etc.).

Simply speaking, conditions of the effectiveness of a confrontational strategy orientation are as follows. The goal should be consolidation of industry, and the key to success should be scale and scope advantages. The company must have better access to resources than typical competitors, because a competitive attack most often causes reaction from other players. A direct attack should hit players in their weak points and have a progressive character – the company should attack a selected, little protected segment, and only after strengthening its position it should move toward further, higher segments and consolidate the industry by means of consecutive acquisitions or forcing competitors to exit.

The second pure orientation is avoidance of competition and creation of a new market. Strategies of Red Bull, IKEA, Nintendo, Atlas, Hilti or Liz Claiborne were directed above all toward the customer. The goal of these companies' strategies was to avoid competition and to reach the customer with an offer that will have a genuine and specific value. Liz Claiborne created elegant business clothes for women; Red Bull – an energy drink surrounded by a mist of mystery and hazard; IKEA – simple and inexpensive furniture; Nintendo made people play computer games, which they had neither time nor willingness to do before; Hilti simplified to the maximum the life of its business partners renting them tools; and Atlas facilitated the task of workers laying tiles. This type of orientation is complementary vis-à-vis the selection of advantage based on relations with customers and most often it has a form of a differentiation. The company can offer a product or a service, which is valued by customers in a specific sense. It visibly differentiates, thanks to such attributes of the offer or model for action, which competitors cannot offer at a given time. The beauty of this advantage is that there are infinitely many bases of differentiation thanks to the enormous variety of needs and customer expectations. The market of watches offers the best example.

It is a simple device, which has one fundamental function – it measures time. This is the core value for a customer, and it might seem that there is nothing more you can think of. But we all know countless watch brands, all offering specific value addition to different groups of customers, and new ones are constantly appearing. The most interesting strategy in this industry was an aggressive attack by Swiss manufacturers passionately conducted in the segment of inexpensive watches. It started in 1983 with the launch of a watch called Swatch (Swiss Watch or Second Watch). The strategy was aimed at creating a new market on a global scale, but it has an indirect element of a competitive battle as Swatch executives claimed: 'We decided to leave the mid-level segment to Seiko and Citizen and dominate the upper and bottom segment, and by doing so close the Japanese in a kind of sandwich.'[18]

Assumptions and strategic goals were truly revolutionary:

- the watches would cost 50 SF maximum; production costs were supposed to equal 15 SF and decrease regularly until they had reached a level of 7 SF (in essence, they were meant to be lower than costs of any competitor in this segment);
- the watch was supposed to be of good quality, waterproof, resistant to shock, with a changeable battery, but not subject to repair;
- sales in the first three years were expected to exceed ten million pieces!

Swatch revolutionized the segment of inexpensive watches not only technologically, but also in terms of marketing and price. The frame of the watch was a created via a precise plastic injection (Swiss engineers created the pattern based on technology used in the manufacturing of plastic toys and bricks), and the mechanical components consisted of an ultra-thin quartz mechanism, Delirium, which was composed of 51 elements (an average mechanism at the time had over 100 parts). It permitted almost complete production automation and cost reduction. Marketing of Swatch is nowadays a classic example. The plastic quartz watches were primarily promoted as unique pieces of modern art, full of color and unexpected design. The marketing strategy by Swatch built its uniqueness based on the following assumptions and programs for action:

- Swatch will be a modern, stylish watch. The tools to reach this goal are the great Italian design by Swatch – full of humor, joie de vivre, color, and also spectacular promotional actions, especially by launching the watch in key markets of the USA and Japan.
- Swatch will be a watch drawing attention and awaking emotions. Every year, two collections including 30 to 70 new models will be launched. Series of particular models will be relatively small (100,000 pieces approximately). Additionally, there will be specialized collections (e.g. sports, ceramic and mechanical), as well as collections signed with names of great designers, which are most often dedicated to great personalities of the world of entertainment and politics in the given year. (Altogether, in the 1980s Swatch launched over 450 models and became a 'cult' watch.) The price of the watch will be high enough to ensure profitability allowing for mass promotion and low enough to make it an impulse purchase.
- The distribution will be mass, but will underline the uniqueness of Swatch compared to watches of other brands, especially Japanese. Swatch watches were sold, for the most part, in shopping malls, boutiques, jewelry stores and stands at airports, avoiding the typical distribution channels of watches such as Timex or Casio. The effect of implementing this strategy resulted in both enormous worldwide success for Swatch and the creation of a new global brand.

High profitability of Swatch allowed the producer, Swiss consortium SMH, to systematically develop the brand. Today, there are five segments and product groups: Swatch Originals (traditional, plastic watches), Swatch Iron (metal watches), Swatch Skin (ultra-thin, approximately 4 mm, earning them a place in the Guinness World Records), Swatch Beat (quartz, promoting the concept of Internet time, which didn't work well) and Swatch Bijoux (jewelry line in cooperation with an Austrian company Swarovski).[19] Another goal of the strategy was the market's consolidation, a process during which Swatch Group overtook other brands, including among others Omega, Tissot, Longines, Breguet, Blancpain, Glashutte Original, Jaquet Droz, Leon Hatot, Tiffany, Rado and improving their position in all upper market segments.

The example of Swatch shows how a company should create an advantage, as well as differentiating dimensions, in order to give its offer a unique character, create a new market and avoid competition. The ulti-mate goal of this strategy is to create a company brand or product brands and link them to customers, ideally for life. Of course, each watch man-ufacturer is constantly seeking such a mini-market to conquer, and this is precisely why every year abounds in new moves aimed at searching for differentiation. For instance, in 2009 Chopard, which supports Elton John's foundation in its fight against AIDS, produced a special series of watches called Elton John. Vacheron Constantin launched a collection called *Les Masques*, a series of watches decorated with ritual masques of tribes from four continents. Van Cleef & Arples, in alliance with D. Baron, a famous enamel painter, created a collection called *Jardins* – a series of watches picturing gardens in enamel. Concorde proposed an ultra-technological watch called C1 Quantum Gravity (with a shiny box for a liquid containing nano-molecules). Baume & Mercier, Corum, Omega, Tudor, Graff and Breitling renew their signature series of sports watches associated with diving, sailing or flying nearly every year in order to maintain customer loyalty.[20] Loyal customers are less sensible to price, allowing companies to maintain high prices (we are speaking about mechanical and electronic watches, where prices can reach sev-eral thousand euros or more) and to reap large profits provided that that their costs are not extraordinarily high!

The third orientation, which links both above orientations, appears most often in practice and is the most difficult. The battle for industry consolidation by means of increasing scale, acquisitions and mergers has a clear logic of cost control discipline. Creating new markets requires passion and an innovative formula for the differentiation advantage. To attempt to achieve both of these at the same time is difficult, because it most often creates a duality of goals – a need to create cost advan-tage and elements of differentiation at the same time. These must be based on sources that competition cannot copy or neutralize, which puts an enormous stress on the effectiveness and efficiency of the busi-ness model. Why do companies choose such a variant? There are at least two good reasons – one practical and one theoretical. From the practical perspective, it is the most natural and obvious option. According to the simplest logic of the market, each company must at the same time fight against competitors and gain customers. Strategic cases like those that created unique markets full of lovers of Cirque du Solei, Apple or A. Rieu Orchestra are and always will be rare. Innovative companies enjoy mar-ket exclusivity for a certain time, but if it is big enough, competitors will unavoidably enter it. That is why most often, the blue ocean is small and the red ocean very large. In practice, a company should constantly strengthen its differentiation-based advantage, and as long as it runs quicker than competitors, it has a chance for better results. As the Red Queen explained to Alice, you must run very fast in order to stay in place.[21] That is why the Red Queen effect became an important fragment of strategy theory, which in practice supports the choice of orientation linking competitive battle with creation of value for customers. Competition is necessary, because it is the basic stimulus in the process of learning and improvement; it is also, apart from customers, the main source of knowledge about logics of the market evolution!

As research shows, stipulations to build a unique, isolated strategic position are, in practice, truly dangerous, in spite of the fact that they sound attractive. Organizations without competitors enjoy the privileges of a monopoly, but inevitably atrophy of the learning process and improvement arrives. It is worth looking at the cases of Liz Claiborne and Polaroid, discussed in other chapters of this book, through this lens. Delayed and limited reactions of these companies to changes in the environment were an indirect effect of the lack of a frequent contact with competitors. Each of these companies had such a unique and coherent strategy that effectively isolated themselves from competitors, but the price they paid was the lack of regular information and feedback from the market and competition. Over a short period, they both won, but in the long run – when the market started to change – this turned out to be extremely harmful.

Another dangerous tendency is being excessively exposed to a large number of differentiated competitors, because it provokes enormous difficulties in the process of building a coherent and effective reaction to various behaviors of these competitors.[22] This is why it is strategically optimal to compete in a modestly differentiated population of competitors and make constant attempts to differentiate position based on this limited pool. Since many managers intuitively know and understand this issue, a market is constantly in a state of dynamic disequilibrium. In practice, instead of stabilizing by means of imitating dominant strategies, as well as through market consolidation, competition constantly rebuilds itself and intensifies as competitors learn from one another and search for an advantage. Some of them are able to create new markets and niches allowing them to have some rest, but soon, this harbor will attract newcomers. The Red Queen effect makes competition a spontaneous process, which is constantly reborn as a result of the process of mutual learning among companies, as well as learning from customers.

Nothing strives for equilibrium – the norm is to constantly recreate the evolutionary disequilibrium. This is why in the long run, each good strategy must take into account both customers and competitors.

Sources of competitive advantage

Competitive advantage has two principal aspects. The first, already discussed, is the type of advantage, about which many interesting typologies have been worked out. The most influential and important is Porter's division into cost advantage and differentiation advantage, which are actually synonyms of basic strategies for action.[23] I have proposed a typology of four types of competitive advantage: natural, the relation of price to performance, service systems and entry barriers, which combined constitute a systemic version of the abovementioned fundamental division.

The second important aspect is the source of advantage, which requires answering the fundamental question: where does company advantage come from? The simplest answer is that competitive advantage can have its source in every process of the strategy's development and execution. It can result from a different interpretation of the company's environment, a different definition of its borders, a different definition of goals and of a unique business model, as well as an appropriate combination of these elements. A competitive advantage can be built either on a precise strength of the company, a process or even an element of the environment or on many resources and capabilities at the same time. In other words – and this differentiation is extremely important in practice – company advantage can have a concentrated or diffused character.[24]

A concentrated advantage resides in a particular precise activity and is best seen in case of natural advantages. Typical examples of this advantage – which exist in the here and now and usually have one precise source – would be based on low cost of workforce of the Chinese textile or shoe manufacturing industry, or local passionate patriotism of breweries' customers or football fans (vide fans of Barcelona, Manchester United or Bayern) or revolutionary patents being the result of an excellent teams of scientists at Novartis, Merck&Co, J&J or Pfizer. A concentrated advantage is easy to achieve, but also easy to understand, because it resides in a particular fragment of the value chain. And understanding is a natural point of departure for imitation and attack from competitors, whose target is to remove the competition's advantage. Obviously, one can improve and defend such an advantage, but it is possible only in cases where the resource constituting the base for advantage fulfills one of the following conditions: either it doesn't wear off (a rare case close to the *perpetuum mobile*) or is difficult to be imitated or replaced (because its development and elaboration takes a long time). That is why theory treats as strategic those resources which are at the same time valuable, rare, difficult to imitate or substitute and appropriately used by the company in its process of developing and executing the strategy.[25]

A diffused advantage has a different logic. It consists in creating an effect (for example, speed of action, high-quality products, good service, customer loyalty, recognizable product brand and good reputation), which appears as a cumulated result of resources and processes of developing a strategy. It is an advantage whose source has a systemic character in the complementarity of resources, processes and strategic choices and resides in the whole value chain. That is why, in practice, a diffused advantage has been illustrated either with a model of a network of dependences or a comb analysis, which facilitates understanding of its logic. A simpler way to show a diffused advantage is a comb analysis, which became extremely popular thanks to the concept of the 'blue ocean'. It is worth to use it as a method, both to formulate as well as to illustrate sources of advantage, because it allows for precise choices. It is enough to have a look at the simplified example of choices needed to build the advantage of a typical supermarket compared to a familiar shop in the neighborhood.

A typical supermarket has a diffused advantage based on several elements at the same time: low prices, wide range of products, location (easy access) and constant product offer. In these areas, which are key for a mass customer, supermarkets have a better position than a typical competitor, and all their systems and functional programs (from IT, selection of suppliers to human resource management) regularly support this advantage creating positive feedback, which is difficult to copy by smaller competitors. A 'familiar' shop in the neighborhood has a natural concentrated advantage, because in its case, key factors are location and quality of service. No supermarket can individualize its service system, that is, welcome the customer in person, know his or her habits, reserve a product for him or her for one day, offer candy to children or simply sell a product without payment in case the customer has forgotten a wallet. That is why supermarkets will never completely make small local shops disappear. Obviously, the problem is that it is ever more difficult to work out an effective business model in the space between a supermarket and a small familiar shop. However, the logic of a diffused and a concentrated advantage allows us to search for a potentially effective strategy in this area. It is known that it is difficult to copy the model of a dispersed advantage of a supermarket, but thanks to the possibility of selecting one of important strategic variables as a new area of concentration, there are many theoretically available models of a concentrated advantage (for example, selling specialized food – healthy, diet, ecological, traditional and exotic).

A diffused advantage is difficult to build and to manage, but it is much more difficult to copy it. Imitation requires duplicating almost all choices and processes, and it actually means creating a copy of the whole company from scratch. Almost no competitor is keen to make such a move because of the obvious reasons.

First, each company has its own worked-out model of action, which permits it to operate in the market and which has created a determined group of customers. An attempt to imitate a systemic competitive advantage doesn't mean a local adjustment, but rather resigning from one's own business model. Such a revolution, in turn, means changing the mental business model, the territory and the technology of action, as well as the relations with customers and suppliers and so on, without any guarantee of success. Additionally, on the way toward change, we can encounter managers' resistance, as well as resistance of employees and investors. One needs to have really good reasons (most often a predicted bankruptcy) in order to take such a revolutionary path.

Second, even if a company decides to make such a desperate move, it is not obvious that it will be able to copy the model of a diffused advantage due to its systemic nature and the lack of precise resources or capabilities. Some global companies have been trying to copy the famous Toyota lean manufacturing model for many years, much the way business schools have been making attempts to create a second Harvard, but no one knows how to do it. We know the logic of choices and the complementing of resources and competences, yet the subtleness of connections worked out over many years effectively protects competitive advantages of strategically managed organizations from direct imitation.

Words are important

Words are not strategy like map is not a territory. But words are important and shape reality. Words are essential for company stakeholders in terms of their understanding of where the company is going and how it wants to operate. That is why a formal strategy formulation, and especially the definition of its goal, territory and competitive advantage, should be carefully agreed on and formulated. The point of departure can be a general strategic hypothesis and an approximate picture of the organization's environment. But in consecutive iterations of analyses and discussions, leaders formulating strategy must set a clear and, if possible, precise goal, as well as develop a model of customer and competitor behavior. Only based on this can they build their own map of the environment, which will make both sense and order. Another move is to determine boundaries of the company operation territory within this environment, as well as to determine the competitive advantage, which will constitute the engine of the strategy. There is no single matrix for this process, but while trying to work out the final formulation there are three helpful tools.

The first is analogy. Many organizations throughout the world have, in the process of developing their strategies by taking the examples of other companies, asked themselves whether they wanted to conduct business in their territories like McDonald's, Lidl (discount retailer), Cemex (innovative Mexican giant on the market of construction materials, especially concrete), Teva (the world's biggest manufacturer of generic medicine) or Vertu (luxurious mobile phones with a limited distribution network). There are also helpful analogies between industries if we want to seek a new advantage, a business model or a financial formula. Some time ago, manufacturers of aircraft engines like Pratt and Whitney or Rolls Royce were selling engines to aircraft companies because they constituted an inseparable part of the aircraft. Today, they hang engines under the wings and sell to airlines hours of engine usage (engine thrust), which is a model of action taken from the sector of services. In another example, Asian Tune Hotels chain models its operations after budget airlines. The hotels are simple, without swimming pools, business centers or restaurants, and guests can choose if they want to pay for extras – from air-conditioning to television and towels. Analogy allows us to sharpen the picture and to more precisely make key choices the company faces, as well as resources and competences indispensable for the choices' realization.

The second tool is comparison with a competitor. Comparison helps determine how and where we can be similar to an important competitor and how we must be different. The goal of strategic benchmarking through comparison with competitors is not simply copying, but making a clear formulation of key differences in our strategy compared to other companies.

The third tool is drawings. As I highlighted several times before, drawing a strategy requires high precision in both choices and relations between them. Comb analyses, net graphs or strategy canvas have become so popular precisely because they are a good way to illustrate key choices, types and sources of competitive advantage and business model. Practice shows that you cannot draw well something you don't understand and which is not relatively simple. The ultimate result of this iterative process should be a concise formulation of the company strategy, at best including all five recommended elements: strategic orientation, principal goal, territory of operations, type of competitive advantage and its sources. Formulation should be simple and coherent, because it is an indispensable feature of every good strategy.

6
What Makes a Good Strategy?

There is always the temptation to build complex models, and that is why academics have a natural tendency to create long lists of strategy characteristics. However, following the wise principle of an English scientist living at the turn of the 13th and 14th centuries, philosopher and theologist William Ockham from the order of Minor Brothers, so-called Ockham razor, one can reduce the number of characteristics of a good strategy to three: simplicity, internal consistency and external coherence (see Figure 6.1). This doesn't mean that every strategy with these factors guarantees an extraordinary company success, because anything can intervene – competitors, government, natural forces and bad luck. It is important, however, to notice that both theory and practice show that these are features that considerably increase the probability of success – both for creating an intellectual concept of strategy and its implementation in a concrete market reality. They are features of a good strategy and they simply mean that the company has developed and implemented a strategy, which maximizes its chances for success. They are also complementary, which means their importance and impact on the final success can be understood only through the interactions between them. Let's start from looking at each of them separately.

Difficult simplicity

The first feature of a good strategy lies in its simplicity, which is well demonstrated in the already-mentioned example of IKEA strategy (see Figure 2.2) – simply a few fundamental choices and a precisely determined goal. Strategy must be simple in its fundamentals, and it must have certain key elements that can be described, and at best, it should be able to be drawn on a simple diagram. Simple does not mean

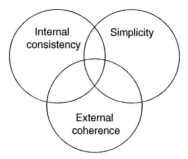

Figure 6.1   Features of a good strategy

easy – simple things can be the most difficult. Cubism in painting, post-modernism in architecture or prose of Charles Bukowski are simple. But it doesn't mean that anyone can paint like Picasso, design buildings like Philip Johnson or sit down and write *Ham on Rye!* The same happens with strategy. Strategy should be simple, but it doesn't mean that its creation and implementation will be easy. On the contrary, the simplest concepts of strategy based on low costs or differentiation are often very difficult, both to develop and implement.

To create its strategy, the whole team of a very successful new banking venture in Poland, Eurobank, needed almost six months. It managed to be successful by means of consecutive experiments and analyses. After the creation process, for many years the strategies for Eurobank or Ryanair have been relatively simple in their assumptions and comprised of a couple of key choices. However, each attempt to imitate these strategies is very difficult, because the key to success is a rigorous implementation on the operational level. There are five key choices in the strategy of Ryanair, but as many as 80 operational programs to reduce costs. The same holds true for the strategy of Nokia, which matured slowly and finally crystalized only in the late 1990s.[1]

Until 1988, the company was growing thanks to mergers and acquisitions and was trying to implement a conglomerate strategy of creating a portfolio, in which there were supposed to be stars (divisions with high profits, but also requiring high investments) and cows (divisions feeding the rest, with lower profits but with a stable positive cash flow). Obviously, the strategy and the implementation weren't very successful, because the period of intensive acquisitions and alliances led to a dramatic financial crisis to such an extent that Nokia was considering selling out to Ericsson. After a period of downsizing and company restructuring, in 1992 Nokia took a decision to concentrate their activities in the telecommunication industry. Consistently over the forthcoming years, the company made other key choices that have shaped its strategy:

- They sold other business lines (some of them very profitable), focusing on the production of telecommunication infrastructure and mobile phones (choice of products);
- They determined the geographic extent of its operations in Europe and then globally (choice of markets);
- They integrated backwards, starting the production of components and electronics, but maintaining a very flexible organizational architecture (choice of business model);
- They built an organizational culture based on four basic values: customer satisfaction, respect for employees, constant learning and ambitions of achievements, and they adjusted to this culture its payroll system, as well as employee assessment (choice of business model);
- They defined the mobile phone as a trendy consumer product, not a technical product (definition of product and market).

Contrary to appearances, the last decision had a strictly strategic character and wasn't easy. It was also a choice against all industry standards and traditions (like the Nintendo's decision concerning the character of the Wii console for computer games). At the beginning of the 1990s Nokia possessed about 12 percent of the world market of mobile phones, but the strategic goal was to double this share. Since main competitors (Siemens, Motorola, Ericsson) disposed of similar technologies and a similar level of expenditure on research and development, it was obvious that Nokia might not achieve its goal in just a simple technological race. In hindsight, it seems obvious, but Nokia was the only one at that time to make the radical choice to redefine a product such as a mobile phone. The project of the key 'Nokia 2100' was handed over to 'freelance' designer Frank Nuovo from Los Angeles (he later became the main designer for Nokia). In 1994, the breakthrough success of this model confirmed the rightness of Nokia's choice and became the source of its great success and a drama for some competitors. No recipe for success lasts forever.

As of 2012 and 2013 Nokia faces the dramatic challenge of finding a new set of choices as the market situation changes. Together with the increasing appeal of smartphones, the entry of new players (Apple with iPhone and Google with Nexus One) and the creation of whole ecosystems of competition present in the market of mobile telecommunication, the importance of the speed of implementing innovation increased enormously. The same holds true for the quality of software, variety of services and ability to cooperate with many complementators present in this market. Nokia was not able to cope with these challenges and its profit garnered in the market of mobile telecommunication decreased from 64 percent in 2007 to 32 percent in 2009 and has been going down since then. No wonder Mary McDowell, a strategist for Nokia, says: 'We have to work faster. We have to improve our action. And we have to combine our products and services better.'[2] In 2010, Nokia opted for a dramatic move to appoint a new CEO. For the first time in the company's history, a foreigner, an American working formerly in Microsoft, Stephen Elop, became Nokia's CEO and it is his and top management's responsibility to rebuild Nokia simplicity out of strategic chaos. And it will be an uphill battle at today's fast changing market.

Searching for simplicity in strategy requires both clarity of strategic choices and clear definition of goals that must be achieved. As D. Collis and M. Rukstad correctly noted, companies often confuse the logic of mission with strategic goal.[3] Mission is a general definition of the sense of the company's existence. Many companies have similar missions. All insurance companies have to ensure financial security to their customers, universities have to educate and telecommunication companies have to connect people. Employees can express these missions with different words, and formal formulations can be either more general or more precise, but their sense remains essentially similar. The strategic goal can include elements of the mission, but it must be firm-specific and measurable. It must be like a highway, on which the company counts miles or kilometers until the final destination.

Strategy simplicity, understood as unambiguity of key choices and goals, is important for at least three reasons. Let's start with the obvious reason – communication. Strategy must be explained to people in order to make them accept it and implement it. And it must be explained to a large group of stakeholders. Suppliers must understand it in order to know what is really important for the company. Each contract, even the most detailed, is incomplete. A simple and clear strategy constitutes an additional message for suppliers to know what they can and should expect from the organization. Strategy communication equals managing expectations.

If the retailer Wal-Mart communicates its strategy through the message 'Low prices, everyday', customers know that they go there to buy cheaper than elsewhere. An enormous range of products, the service and convenient location constitute an additional support for this message, but low price is the key. The famous statement of the shipping company Federal Express: 'Absolutely. Positively. Overnight.' expressed both the essence of the company service (overnight shipment) and constituted a message for customers and employees, saying what the most important part of the strategy is. Employees are key addressees of the message concerning strategy, because they are the ones to implement it and see its results. That is why communicating the strategy to employees should highlight the unequivocal goal, extent and methods of acting. No one can understand a 100-page document or a presentation of 80 slides illustrating the strategy, or even if someone does, it will be difficult to accept it, remember it and explain it to subordinates.

Apart from suppliers, customers and employees, in case of public companies we also have to count on the opinion of shareholders and analysts. For them, transparency of the company equals not only availability of data but also transparency of the strategy. They can agree to a given strategy or not, but in order to maintain a dialog with them managers need to define the strategy clearly. It is not easy to understand a corporate strategy that has many projects and many dimensions. For instance, if one takes almost any large petrochemical company's publically stated strategy, it contains almost everything: organic and nonorganic growth, effectiveness improvement, consolidation, progress, synergy, wholesale and retail market expansion, domestic and international market expansion, further implementation of the strategy of two brands, launch of research and extraction works etc. Of course, these corporations must perform most of these tasks; however, this is by no means a strategy, but rather a list of all possible important actions the company wants to carry out. Second, this kind of message doesn't say what the company really considers to be its strategic goal and priorities. We also deal with many other types of stakeholders – from government agencies to nonprofit organizations of all sorts, who, having a stake in the effects and operational methods of a given company, want to understand its strategy. A clearly communicated strategy to all stakeholders is a certain antidote to the complexity of today's company and the very process of management. The world of organizations and management isn't simple. It has been complicated by new technologies of production, distribution, accounting, IT and the necessity of managing ever more demanding and mobile personnel. All this takes place with growing speed in conditions of market globalization and complex legal and administrative regulations. Complexity is like a powerful virus – there is no good medicine against it. That is why in the world of complexity, companies particularly need clarity and simplicity of choices concerning what to strive for and how to do it. My personal test for simplicity and communicativeness of strategy has been the same for many years – a good strategy can be drawn on one sheet of paper.

Simplicity is needed also for another reason rarely discussed in books on strategy – a simple strategy is necessary to build a good incentive system. Strategy can have a very motivating impact, because it creates a loop of a positive feedback. It liberates employee ambitions, giving them a chance to have their efforts and commitment rewarded, thus motivating them to act. Starting from the beginning, simplicity and unambiguity of choices facilitate appropriate allocation of the organization's two most important resources – time and attention of managers and employees. P. Drucker wrote about it 50 years ago, and his words are just as valid today as when he argued that in order to get economic results, management should focus their attention on the few areas of activity that can bring important economic results.[5] It is obvious that the more issues are treated as strategic, the more difficult focus and motivation are. The company starts to be everything for everyone. That is when managers devote time and attention to urgent matters, losing sight of fundamental issues. It entirely destroys any incentive system, because there is a tension between what is important, what is measured, what is assessed and what is rewarded. Only a relatively simple strategy allows the linkage of these elements coherently, because it concentrates attention on a few priorities that can be measured, assessed and linked to strong or weak material and symbolic stimuli, depending on what the organization decides to use.

Another important aspect, related to the incentive system, of the dependence between strategy simplicity and motivation is the selection of employees. Theoretically, we know that the kind of employees the company hires will be of fundamental importance for their motivation, but in practice, we often forget what J. Roberts underlines: 'Whom the firm attracts and selects as employees can have a tremendous effect on their motivation. Clearly, it should seek to attract people who are interested or challenged by the work being done. This is intuitively clear – if people like their work, there is less of a problem motivating them. More formally, this sort of matching reduces the divergence of interests that underlies the motivation problem. Also it is clearly advantageous to match people with rewards that can be offered. For example, if it is desirable to provide intense incentives but performance measures are not very precise or results are hard to forecast, then it is important that the people put in these jobs not be too risk-averse. If only non-monetary incentives can be offered, then get people who value the rewards that are possible'.[6]

Wal-Mart and Intel have different strategies, and they should hire different people. What counts in Wal-Mart is operational excellence, everyday methodical search for economies and friendly attitude to customers. Intel fights in an extremely unpredictable market, at the same time adapting its products and experimenting with the newest technologies, which requires stable cooperation of people from all company areas, acceptance of risks and readiness to experiment.

Differing market strategies were adopted by two new Polish banks, Eurobank and Alior Bank. Eurobank was extremely concentrated on one or two products (mainly consumer loans) and started on a limited scale, assuming an aggressive growth. Alior Bank started from the beginning with a full range of products (all banking products, both for individual and institutional customers) on a relatively large scale thanks to high capitalization, which Eurobank didn't have. It can therefore afford a balanced, systematic growth. Both banks chose good incentive systems and appropriate people who fit their respective strategies. Eurobank hired very young employees, for whom it was often the first workplace, and used an aggressive incentive system linked to the sales volume of consumer loans. Alior Bank hired people with at least a couple of years of experience in banking, for whom it was a consecutive workplace (but for many the first encounter with entrepreneurship), and applied a balanced incentive system linked to the general results of particular establishments. A strong correlation between strategy, employee selection and incentive system leads to another positive effect apart from the concentration of efforts and commitment, namely self-selection. Employees who don't care for a given strategy or a given incentive system will play with the system and eventually leave the company in a natural way; those who feel motivated stay.[7] You cannot build a common culture and commitment among people who are completely different and have different goals and needs. A certain element of selection and self-selection is necessary for the company to be able to become a community of people who collaborate together and have common language, passion and values, and appreciate mutual cooperation. It is a priceless element of effective strategy implementation.

Third, strategy simplicity facilitates precise definition of company architecture, as well as resources and competences indispensable for its practical realization. Two of the most popular organizational structures – functional and divisional – are good examples of configurations corresponding to different strategies. In the functional structure, people cooperate within their functions in a natural way – research and development, procurement, production, sales, service, finance or human resource management. This is where communities of people with similar education, norms, behaviors and standards of excellence appear, and it is not at all easy to find for them a common platform for understanding with other professional communities. A functional structure will be a natural choice of company architecture when the organization has one key function and develops its resources and competences. In high-tech companies, it is often the research and development department, and at distribution firms, the logistics department. Other departments become supporting departments, and it couldn't be otherwise. That is why such a combination is the best in small and medium companies. Hierarchy is complemented with common culture, everyday natural contact between employees and good insight of management into the entity of the company's operations, which allows a company to ensure equilibrium and harmony, which are indispensable for cooperation. In big companies this is practically impossible, and a functional division simply doesn't work there even if it would be the most logical solution. That is why all big companies in the world are organized into divisions, most often according to markets or products.

In the 1990s, an extreme solution was the case of the European industrial conglomerate Asea Brown Boveri, which was divided into almost 100 independent product units. Each of them constituted a separate legal body and had its own balance sheet and income statement. Each big corporation uses a slightly different design, but all are divided into smaller parts. Thanks to that, the company is simplified and can develop reasonable local strategies for action, measures of effectiveness and systems of assessment, specific for each business.

Acer, a Taiwanese manufacturer of computers, globalizing its operations, divided into over 40 independent divisions, which were assembling computers adjusted to local needs. Swedish manufacturer of energy, Vattenfall, opts for a geographical division into markets of Belgium, The Netherlands and Luxembourg, Central Europe and Scandinavia as well as technology division according to the way of producing energy (wind, nuclear, traditional).

Henkel, a German manufacturer of detergents and chemicals, divides into three separate product lines: washing powders and domestic chemical products, cosmetics and industrial adhesives. They have a common mission (*'make people's life easier, better and more beautiful'*), but different strategic goals and separate structures. What is more, each product group has its regional territorial structures. It is difficult to expect Henkel not to divide production and sales of its industrial adhesives and washing powders into separate divisions – their value chains and communities of employees are almost entirely separate. There are obviously issues that link this corporation into one entity. It has a homogeneous system of reporting and information (SAP), a common policy of human resource management, a common brand. Henkel is a typical example of the dominant structural solution today, *front-end-back-end.* Some activities are organized functionally and remain a 'central background' of the company, whereas bundles of actions, which are key for the strategy's realization, are organized according to regions/markets/products and constitute the 'front' of the corporation. It is a structural attempt to achieve balance between the centralized usage of common resources of the corporation, the improvement of functional competences and the constant adaptation on local markets.[8]

Apart from structural decisions, the strategy's execution also requires development of an appropriate configuration of resources and competences. When a company doesn't have such resources and competences, the problem of strategy is intellectually simple. You need to acquire, purchase or shape these resources and competences. However, the strategic problem of many companies is not that they don't have resources and competences, but that they have too many of them. Companies are often like basements or attics in old houses – full of objects, equipment, boxes, trash and souvenirs gathered over many years. With time, each company becomes a great source of dispersed assets and knowledge, which no one controls. In this situation, a true challenge is to define key company competences. What are we really able to do best? What are we able to do better than others? Why are we able to do it? And finally the key question – do we use these capabilities in practice? These are very difficult questions that started the already-discussed theory of competitive advantage, understood as a set of key resources and capabilities (Resource Based View – RBV).[9]

If strategy is very complex, defining key resources and competences from the point of view of future success becomes problematic. It is even more challenging to understand how these resources and capabilities should be configured and linked in order to make them complementary. When strategy is simple, the answer to the question, 'what resources and competences are necessary for its execution?' is not trivial, but the search for the answer to this is much better directed. Therefore, strategy gurus often recall the maxim about a fox and a hedgehog from the poem of a Greek poet, Archiloch – 'a fox knows many little things, and a hedgehog one, but a big one'. Companies with a good strategy know one big thing well – which resources and capabilities are key for strategy implementation – and can adjust the company architecture to this knowledge.

Internal consistency

Another rule of a good strategy is internal consistency.[10] A good strategy requires strategic choices and functional programs to be mutually complementary and supportive. Speaking in a systemic way, they should create a positive feedback loop. It means that each choice and each way of its realization has to strengthen effectiveness (productivity) of the remaining choices and actions.[11] In economic terms, choices should complement each other. Speaking in a colloquial way, all pistons must be synchronized.

Internal consistency of strategy concerns both conceptual strategic choices themselves, as well as linking these choices with company programs for action: hierarchical functioning of information and decision flow, incentive systems, structural division of tasks and all coordination routines. Let's start with a challenge of consistency of key choices themselves. Choices by IKEA are consistent and strengthen each other, such as with locations of shops, a product range that maximizes rotation (high percentage are their own brands) and low prices in discounters like Aldi or Lidl. Most often these choices concern a couple of basic strategic elements – type of customer, type of product, importance of the brand, quality and price, distribution technology, way of management. Between choices, which are in an obvious way either coherent or conflicting, there is a range of choices allowing the creation of interesting and often innovative strategic combinations. We don't know a priori how many combinations there are, for which you can find a place on the market, but it is a limited number.

A good example of a set of simple and consistent choices is Ryanair, which changed its strategy after the financial collapse in 1991 and became a discount airline. It competes on the market of air transport with extremely low prices, but at the same time it gets the highest margins in the industry. It means that it effectively achieves the goal of minimizing costs thanks to a couple of key choices. First, it uses only standard aircrafts, Boeing 737s, which decreases costs of purchase, service and recruitment of pilots. Second, it maximizes rotation of the most expensive assets in the world, flying often and minimizing to 30–45 minute stops at airports. Third, passenger services are limited almost to zero, and each element of good service is paid for additionally. Fourth,

Ryanair constantly grows and creates new connections, whereas economy of scale decreases both its fixed costs per passenger or employee and the intensity of competition – for every connection, other competitors fall out. Lack of any service accompanying the basic offer for transport from A to B, simplicity and minimalist configuration of the company constitute the essence of strategy of cost leadership allowing for extremely low prices of air tickets. Obviously, such an offer effectively attracts young people seeking price promotions, and at the same time discourages passengers seeking at least minimal comfort, service and guarantee of further connections while traveling.[12]

Another interesting company, Shanghai Zhenhua Port Machinery, is a dominant player in the world market of port cranes. It has a clearly defined market – reloading ports, and a clearly defined product – cranes. Instead of following the typical path, investing in research and development and concentrating on new technologies and product innovations, the company was seeking another coherence. Structurally and procedurally, it directed the attention of its almost one thousand engineers and constructors toward reduction of costs of construction and production of modular cranes (already a very expensive equipment), which allows the quick adjustment of standard cranes to meet the functional needs of concrete reloading ports.[13]

The situation of inconsistent choices is equally clear and very frequent in practice. You cannot create a discount airline with well-developed customer service and a small scale of operations. A fashionable clothes company cannot at the same time quickly react to changes in customer tastes, limit the number of designers to zero and outsource production to China. These are incoherent choices and any attempt to realize them creates conflicts and frustration. Theoretically and practically, there is an unlimited set of incoherent choices, whereas the number of coherent combinations is limited. Therefore, we deal with an infinite number of bad strategies and a limited number of really good ones.

The second challenge is the search for consistency between strategic choices and reality of the company's routines and operations. Precise programs for action, from marketing to human resource management, have to constitute a logical implementation of key choices, as well as support and complement each other in a rigorous way. One cannot offer modern products and services of high quality with old equipment, an underinvested development department and high rotation of poorly paid personnel. One needs to take the example of the McDonald's business model seriously – strategic choices linked to product offer, prices and system of fast service are supported with rigorous training of temporary personnel, careful selection of suppliers, absolute standardization of all aspects of operations, optimal location and arrangement of outlets, rigorous control of costs and mass marketing. All pistons are synchronized – each procedure and each aspect of operations is subject to optimal realization of strategic choices, and the effect is noticeable. It is enough to go to any given restaurant section in a modern shopping mall around the world and have a look at queues in front of fast food joints. All of them offer similar food, but the longest queues are almost always in front of McDonald's. A consistent strategy is really effective, even when offered products or services are substandard in terms of real quality.

A model example of internal consistency of choices and programs for action is the McKinsey & Company. Its strategy is based on three consistent choices. The company offers: (1) strategic consulting (2) for top management of big companies and (3) operation on a global scale. The justification of such choices is very simple – it is a prestigious domain, very profitable and intellectually very interesting for consultants. In order to fulfill these choices in practice, McKinsey concentrates on three internal programs for action, which also constitute key competences of the company. The first is a systematic acquisition of very good employees, which is not easy, because you need to find people linking many talents at the same time. They must be very intelligent and creative human beings, able to work hard over long periods. They must also be ready for constant learning and innovation, and at the same time accept the anonymity of consulting projects. Some of these features are conflicting, others are difficult to be assessed a priori, but a consulting company must be able to find these people among thousands of candidates. And since employee rotation, even where the work is interesting, is quite significant, the company must constantly 'feed' itself with new, strongly motivated employees. Another competence and program of the company is to create effective project teams. In spite of the existence of great literature concerning this topic, it is hard to build effective teams, and creating teams of aggressive and intelligent professionals is even harder.[14] Finally, the last capability is to develop, based on individual, differentiated projects, effective consulting standards, which can later be used nearly on a mass scale. Each project is slightly different and has its specification and a consulting company is not able to realize effectively unique projects starting each time from zero. Consulting companies constitute a team of craftsmen, not an association of artists. Therefore, a very important capability is creation of standards (*templates*, as it is called in jargon), which can be applied in various environments and countries, as well as accumulation and stan-dardization of knowledge from previous consulting projects. It is a great challenge, which McKinsey executes better than most other consult-ing companies. On one hand, it devotes relatively large resources (IT, separate consulting teams, training and time of consultants realizing projects) to the achievement of this goal, but on the other hand, it carefully motivates consultants to share their real knowledge, and not simply hundreds of pages of reports or PowerPoint presentations.

The essence of consistency, as the above examples and discussion show, is complementarity of choices and actions.[15] For the sake of sim-plification, let's assume that the leader developing a strategy makes two basic choices (or actions). From an economic point of view, their complementarity means that one choice results in the increase of attrac-tiveness of the other one. Remaining in a positive feedback loop, they mutually strengthen each other's effectiveness, which is typically illus-trated by the example of the relation between product quality and product price. Classical complementary choices are basic quality and low price or high quality and high price. That is why, among others, contemporary markets usually have a bipolar character.[16] The situation of companies in upper segments is good, because it is obvious that you need to achieve consistency of choices of high prices, high quality, high technologies, professional workforce and so on. The situation of compa-nies in the large, mass bottom segments is also good, because the keys to their success are production scale, mass technology of production and standardization. It is difficult to achieve consistency in the middle of the market pyramid, because a firm has to solve dilemmas and con-flicts existing between inconsistent choices in an innovative way, for example, limited scale of operations and low costs.

One of the best-described examples of complementarity in strategy practice and its dilemmas is the case of Liz Claiborne, manufacturers of women's fashion apparel.[17] The company was founded in 1976 and 15 years later it had a turnover of over two billion dollars and the high-est return on equity (over 40%) among all Fortune 500 companies. Liz Claiborne exactly fit the basic demographic trend of the 1980s – women in the USA went to work, but didn't have anything to wear. There was simply no 'business outfit' for women, thus it was exactly around this niche that the company decided to build their position and brand. The whole strategy of the company was composed of a couple of key choices. The first concerned the design. Every typical season, the com-pany offered four to seven collections of classic elegant sweaters, jackets, blouses, skirts, dresses and trousers in various colors. Prices of these products were relatively high, and collections of Claiborne had great added value for working women for two reasons: the logic of a limited number of collections and the colors facilitated shopping. At the same time, clothes were not becoming obsolete fast, because you could combine them freely. Colors didn't change over years, blue remained the same blue, green remained the same green and black remained black. Consumers could match colors of clothes bought two years earlier with a piece from the last season and still match perfectly.

The second important choice of Liz Claiborne concerned selling whole collections and presenting them as entities in elegant shopping malls. Instead of allowing retailers to choose concrete product lines, the company was exclusively selling the entire collection (not only of clothes but also cosmetics, shoes and bags), in appropriate proportions of colors and products, requiring from retailers dedicated space and coverage of costs of the whole initiative (which was revolutionary at the time). Indeed, for the sake of strategy, Liz Claiborne defined their product to be the entire collection, and thanks to this got its 'shops in shops'. Its designers and consultants took care of the physical aspect and attractiveness, regularly ensuring shops new designs and business support. On the territory of 'its' shops, the company also organized presentations and various marketing events, which was raising its presence and highlighting the novelty of collections in shops as well as eliminating the need for expensive, mass marketing campaigns in mass media.

Third, Liz Claiborne had a unique sales technology – it sold collections from the company's headquarters in New York exclusively, a process carried out by a team of almost a hundred salespersons. Competitors selling to shopping malls had to go with samples of products to each individual client's headquarters to meet with buyers from textile departments. Meanwhile, by centralizing the process of sales, Liz Claiborne ensured contacts on the highest level of management. Because of the presentation's location, as well as the typical contract volume, the company was most often visited by each retailer's top management. Additionally, the company was maintaining production on a level slightly below orders, increasing customer loyalty (or switching costs in economic terminology). Fourth, almost the entire production process was outsourced to Asia, which lowered costs and permitted prices to remain on a moderate level.

All choices by Liz Claiborne were complementary and strengthened the company effectiveness. Customers could appreciate the product only when it was presented as an entity. It was possible because, thanks to sales of collections in New York, Liz Claiborne made sure that purchasing decisions were taken in the top-management level. Managers of retailers trusted the company because it was offering consulting support as far as arrangement of shop windows and shop space were concerned, and it was delivering attractive collections six times per year, which was more often than its competitors. Both the company and shopping malls had worthy margins due to the outsourcing of production to countries with low costs of workforce. Limiting supply decreased the risk of collection failure – both from a company and retailer perspective. The company's strong brand position guaranteed constant orders from demanding customers, which in turn limited shopping malls' readiness to question policies applied by Liz Claiborne. On the whole, the company's strategy led to the creation of positive feedback – each choice strengthened the rest, and the whole system of operations worked effectively for the benefit of Liz Claiborne and its business partners until a crisis hit.

In the 1990s, a couple of trends in the environment provoked a dramatic decrease in the effectiveness of this strategy. Companies started to allow employees to wear less formal clothes, which decreased the demand for classic, elegant business clothes by Liz Claiborne. Shopping malls were forced to lower costs, facing a full frontal attack by discount hypermarkets such as Wal-Mart, Kmart or Target. They started to demand price reductions from suppliers and fast product rotation and were much less keen to meet requirements concerning the purchase of entire collections. Thanks to new information and production technologies, competitors were offering much faster production cycles, faster than Liz Claiborne could react to demand changes. Liz Claiborne wasn't ready for the new market situation. Its system of operations was internally consistent, but highly inflexible. It required long cycles of preparing and producing goods, sales of entire collections and a strong support of retail. Besides, it depended on cooperation with many small manufacturers in Asia, who didn't invest in either IT systems or in systems of production allowing for a faster execution of orders. Changing one of the strategy's elements wasn't actually possible without changing the rest of them. During the period of success, the company gathered considerable surpluses of cash (500 million dollars approximately), so instead of adapting and changing its strategy, it used its financial resources to increase stocks and accelerate the reaction to demand changes. Obviously, such a situation couldn't last long, and since money was disappearing, the company changed its board of management. The new leader, Paul Charron, and his team (he effectively changed the whole top management) have radically changed the company's choices in the area of design, sales, marketing and production, and developed a new business model, better adjusted to the fast-changing environment.

As the example of Liz Claiborne shows, even the best solutions have negative side effects, and the strategy's internal consistency creates two long-term important limitations of organizational effectiveness in areas of learning and adaptation. The process of organizational learning takes place according to a simple sequence: variation – selection – retention. The point of departure of learning by people and companies is the same. It is availability and variety of new stimuli. It means readiness to search the environment, gather new information and experiment. A company with highly consistent internal choices, like Liz Claiborne, with time loses such readiness. Experimenting with consistent choices doesn't make sense – partial changes lead to decreased effectiveness. The company stops reacting to new stimuli and signals from the environment. The more the strategy is consistent and effective, the more autistic the company becomes with time. In case of lack of new stimuli (psychologists call this phenomenon a sensorial deprivation), the process of learning is almost impossible – there is no substance to learn.

The second stage is selection – the choice from many possibilities and solutions created by the company's own experiments and observations of the surrounding reality, concepts and types of actions better than the previous ones. It requires openness to new opportunities and capability of conducting a balanced assessment of available alternatives. The example of Liz Claiborne illustrates exactly why it is difficult. Change and adaptation of consistent strategic choices to the important environmental changes demand radical transformation of the company's business model because local adjustments do not work.

The third stage is retention, that is, the choice of a certain opportunity and its diffusion within the organization. The whole process of learning is regularly strengthened or weakened – solutions, which turn out to be good (the company is 'rewarded' with high effectiveness) are adopted and others are rejected. If consistency of choices and routines simply blocked or facilitated the cycle of organizational learning process, the situation would be trivial. Unfortunately, theory and research show that the situation is more complex. Neither consistency nor inconsistency makes the variation – selection – retention process a fast and efficient learning cycle.[18]

Organizational consistency decreases variety of potential stimuli, because it decreases readiness to experiment and observe the experience of other companies. Simply speaking, it creates cognitive filters. It also both facilitates and makes reasonable selection difficult. It facilitates it, because the number of new solutions, which will be consistent with the ones the organization has previously applied, is limited. It makes it difficult, because choices and procedures that are more effective than previous ones will be difficult to be approved and executed. Finally, it facilitates reception and diffusion of new solutions within an organization once it accepts and treats them as its own.

Lack of consistency creates its own difficulties in learning and implementing changes. It facilitates process of generating new solutions, but has a negative impact on selection, as it makes assessment of solutions difficult from the point of view of effectiveness and retention, because particular organization units have different logic of operations. This situation creates an important problem for many organizations. Because of the lack of a correct diagnosis, these kinds of situations often contribute to company instability or even decline. The learning process is an indispensable component of long-term success; internal consistency and stability of choices constitute an indispensable element of an effective strategy implementation. It is, however, difficult to have both of them simultaneously. If the environment becomes more dynamic and learning and innovativeness are important for the company's survival and success, managers need to deliberately decrease the consistency of key choices and procedures, or even to divide the organization into parts. In turn, if the environment becomes stable again, managers can strengthen internal adjustment in order to maximize effectiveness.

Since the speed of environmental changes fluctuates, the organization faces a difficult choice concerning whether and how to manipulate the level of internal adjustment. If it decides to do it regularly, at each possible moment it can act less effectively than it would be optimal, but it increases its adaptation capabilities and chances for long-term high effectiveness. If it decides to do it periodically, every now and then it will face a smaller or larger, but always expensive, revolution. This was the case of McDonald's, whose totally consistent choices and procedures have ensured extraordinary results for many years, at the same time making it difficult to learn and change. In the 1980s and 1990s, the company understood that it must start to adapt to changes in the environment (even in the US, the hamburger stopped being the only food), but it did this according to its dominant centralized logic. It experimented with centrally led experiments that were contrary to the original strategy, mainly with the product offer (salads, soups, pizza and the famous diet hamburger, McLean Deluxe). The crisis the company faced at the end of the 1990s provoked a strategic change – a decrease of internal consistency, in order to increase ability of regions and countries to experiment locally with the menu (it is different, although similar, in the US, Poland and China) as well as marketing and recruitment policies. Another issue is how McDonald's will handle possible accusations of being at least partially responsible for the obesity of millions of people around the world. But this is a problem of adaptation to changes in the environment, which is strongly connected to the third feature of a good strategy – external coherence.

External coherence

The last rule of a good strategy is its external coherence. Contrary to common opinion, true innovation, especially generating completely new products, rarely pays off. The majority of innovators end badly, because they are ahead of their times. Pneumatic tires were created in 1845 by Robert W. Thompson, a modern equivalent of a car was created by Stanley brothers at the end of the 19th century, a tape recorder by V. Paulsen in 1899, a helicopter by Juan de la Cierva in 1930, Internet sale of books by Charles Stack and a video player by a company called Ampex. Apple was neither the first to develop a system to download music files, nor the mini music player. Before iTunes and iPod, we had Napster and MP3 players were produced by Multimedia (a player called Rio) and by Best Data (a player called Cabo 64). But does anyone even remember them today? Markides and Geroski in their analysis of the fate of innovators indicate a cruel truth: 'Both individuals and companies that *create* new markets are not necessarily the ones that *scale* them up into big mass markets. Indeed, the evidence shows that in the majority of cases, the early pioneers of radically new markets are almost never the ones that scale up and conquer those markets.'[19]

A genuine innovation of strategy means it's a good adjustment to market trends, demographic changes, behavior of companies and people and general changes in the environment. As stated earlier, a good strategy has an element of passion, which permits production at the junction of analysis and the imagining of a set of possible scenarios – strategy's hypotheses. Some of them may be aligned to present market states, others can go ahead of the market, but one needs to be careful in order not to totally 'overshoot' the market, proposing an offer too ahead of customer expectations in a given segment, like Apple did with its Newton. Though it didn't repeat the same mistake with iPod, complemented with iTunes. Pioneers often end with an arrow in their backs (it makes sense to watch old Western movies!), and that is why many companies seek external coherence of their strategies, observing failures and successes of entrepreneurs – great market experimenters.

A good example of coherent strategies would be the successes of some Polish entrepreneurs in the turbulent market that was formed in the 1990s. One of the most successful entrepreneurial ventures in Poland is the already-mentioned Atlas SA, the third largest European producer of construction chemicals: adhesives, ready-to-use mortars, floors and self-leveling subfloors, insulation and sealing materials and so on.[20] Its flagship product – a special type of adhesive for laying ceramic and stone tiles – was simple and could be produced by any manufacturer. The only indispensable tangible asset was a mixer of concrete. The market at the beginning of 1990s was dominated by the German company Henkel and was complemented with mass imports from virtually everywhere, carried out by thousands of entrepreneurial distributors. Hence, the product was simple and the market very difficult. An innovative strategic idea by Atlas consisted in a careful observance of the market and noticing that apart from a great chance created by immense demand (everyone was building a house and laying ceramic tiles!), the basic market problem was the bad habits of Polish tile craftsmen used to the traditional cement-calcareous mortar.

Atlas, using all available information channels, started an immense advertising and educational campaign of the ready-sticking mortar, specially created for laying ceramic tiles. The first one was simply the bag, on which the instruction for use has been placed. However, it turned out that nobody read what was written on bags. Therefore Atlas printed almost 200,000 leaflets with an illustrated instruction for use, and enclosed the leaflet with its products as well as distributed them in selling points. The second channel were producers of ceramics whom Atlas convinced to develop a joint four-page instruction, which was enclosed to ceramic tiles they were selling. One half of the instruction described qualities of ceramic tiles as construction material, and the other half explained how to apply Atlas's adhesive in order to place and stick them. The third channel were distributors of Atlas, whom the company carefully selected and supported with heavy promotion in regional newspapers that regularly published promotional texts informing about both the use of the mortar and where to buy it.

Both manufacturers of ceramics and distributors became those who, in today's strategy theory, are called 'complementators'. The success of Atlas favored their success (sales were growing) and their success favored the success of Atlas, which additionally increased external coherence between the company's strategy and environmental trends. The fourth channel became editors and journalists dealing with the topic of construction, whom Atlas convinced to feature its products and strategy, preparing specialized cycles of articles including illustrations, pictures and ready solutions.

Coherence between Atlas and trends and phenomena in the company's environment was multidimensional. First, the company simply leveraged the enormous potential demand and made an alliance with manufacturers of ceramic tiles who had a stake in its success. Second, it efficiently used a dispersed distribution network based on small Polish firms to create economies of scale, as well as install the loyalty of distributors. Third, it conducted an immense educational campaign to make the company's offer coherent with customer expectations. The last element building this coherence became the concept of converting Atlas into a national, almost patriotic brand. To achieve such status, Atlas chose the stork for its symbol, a bird widely considered by Poles to be the most 'Polish' of all. The choice of this bird and, in this way, underlining the 'Polishness' of the product were coherent with the awakening national pride, the feeling that 'Poles can do it', and that Polish products could match Western products in terms of quality. Purchasing Atlas's glue became an almost patriotic move, and the advertisement slogan added in 1999, 'I love Poland', further strengthened Polish people's affinity for the company.[21]

Another good example of such coherence is TZMO SA. TZMO became a domestic champion in the Polish market, and then managed to conquer the Central European and Russian market of feminine hygiene products with its flagship brand, Bella. The essence of TZMO strategy's external coherence, especially at the beginning of the 1990s, was concentration on the largest bottom-market segment, while Procter & Gamble and other foreign multinationals were building their brands and product awareness in upper segments with intensive advertising campaigns. Traditional markets have a shape of a pyramid, and TZMO effectively used the fact that the largest scale can be achieved by dominating the bottom of the pyramid with good, simple and inexpensive products. Later, the company applied the same strategic logic in Ukraine and Russia, becoming a market leader in each of these markets.

Even global corporations, for which the world constitutes a natural market, try to reconcile integration of actions carried out within the whole company with local adjustment of the strategy. Some time ago these strategies were described with a slogan 'Think globally, act locally', because the basic strategy consisted in an intelligent replication of one model of action on a world scale. But the markets of the US, Germany, China or Poland have always been and will always be different. That is why clever corporations give their local leaders space to build external coherence with the local market.

The effect of such decentralization of thinking and acting is very advantageous for international companies, because today, local developing markets constitute a great source of interesting innovations. They are simply more diverse and dynamic than mature markets, and this diversity constitutes substance for change. Companies, which start to understand it, quickly resign from primitive replications of strategies, where the company simply overtakes the business model (or product) developed in the US or Germany and implements it with small modifications in Poland, Russia, India or China. An outstanding company, Google, didn't want to adapt its business model to the Chinese market and lost this market to the local competitor Baidu, who has a more local model of action and offered, among others, options of downloading films and music free of charge, which is popular in China.[22]

Another American company, General Electric, shows greater adaptation ability in its strategy for action. In May 2009, while searching for new sources of growth, it announced a six-year program for creating over 100 innovative products and services in the area of healthcare. What is an absolute novelty in GE's strategy, and what will constitute an example to follow by many MNCs, is that the majority of these innovations are developed in emerging markets as a result of adaptations to local conditions, and only then they are transferred onto mature markets. Two examples of such products are a handy, compact electrocardiograph created in India and a small PC-compatible ultrasonograph created for the benefit of rural markets in China.[23] It is a reversal of the typical sequence, which has dominated for many decades and which consisted in moving products developed in mature markets eventually to less developed markets!

The quality of external adjustment comes, similar to internal consistency, with a price. The price is the limited ability of adaptation. If we treat the requirement of external coherence in an extremely rigorous way, we can state that there is only one good strategy understood as an optimal adjustment in a given environment. The issue becomes complicated if we recall the previous requirement – the one of internal strategy consistency. Each set of internally adjusted choices will be, per definition, slightly differently adjusted to the external environment. You cannot simply manipulate internal links a little bit in order to adjust the company better to its environment, because internal consistency has its logic and its inertia. To explain this, let's look for a while at the logic of two coherent production systems, which constantly coexist in the market: a traditional system of mass production and a modern, flexible, so-called lean system. To make the issue as simple as possible, selected features of these systems can be presented, following J. Roberts, in the following way.[24]

System of mass production demands specialized machinery; long production runs; infrequent product changes; narrow product lines; mass marketing; limited worker skills and specialization; central expertise and coordination; hierarchical planning and control; vertical internal communication; sequential product development; static optimization; accent of volumes and so. On the other hand, the system of flexible production has very different logic. It demands flexible machines; low set-up costs; short production runs; frequent product improvements; broad product lines; targeted markets; highly skilled and cross-trained workers; accent on quality and costs; worker initiative; local information and self-regulation; horizontal communication; cross-functional development teams and so forth.

Both systems, constituting important element of organizational strategies, are reasonable: both are coherent and have their own different logic. The first was more effective and dominant some time ago, mainly because of slow changes in the industrial environment. That is why many companies have made it a key element of their strategies and have built distribution and marketing systems around it. These strategies were shaped by mass markets of the 20th century – from steel to car production, clothes and food. But as market segmentation and customer differentiation grew, the logic of an effective strategy started to change. It required both scale and offer differentiation, and the answer was the system of flexible production, which is more effective in many industries. In this sense, it is an optimal strategy, but it doesn't mean that all companies will want to and will be able to adapt it.

First, even in the most dynamic environment, a company can find niches, where the system of mass production will still be effective and some companies will decide to apply it as a fragment of their strategies. The second reason for sticking to a given set of mass production choices is the fact that a change in production system demands a radical change. There is no possibility of an incremental, partial passage, because both systems constitute consistent, but dramatically different, conceptual and practical solutions. The hybrid is most often inconsistent and less effective than any of these systems separately. That is why managers of a company using a system of mass production, even of effectiveness lower than the one of a flexible lean system, can accept it as the second best solution in order to decrease costs and risks of transformation from one production pattern to another.

It was exactly what managers of American car companies did facing a threat from Japanese manufacturers. The strategy and the supporting production system of Japanese companies in the 1990s were evidently better and more effective. However, their implementation in American firms would have required such a revolution on the cognitive and cultural level – a transformation of relations with suppliers and customers and the whole management system – that managers decided to constantly improve their less effective mass production system instead of changing it. Maybe they hoped that with time and by means of improvements and investments, the old system would become as effective as the flexible one. That is why they spent billions of dollars for automation of plants, implementation of quality circles, elements of *kaizen*, programs of organizational culture and information systems of rapid reaction development. They even undertook experiments with new business models, the most famous being a division of GM that produced and sold a small car, Saturn, which competed with economical cars of Japanese companies.[25]

Such operations and adjustments, conducted for approximately 20 years, turned out to be almost sufficient, in the sense that they allowed them to control the pace at which American companies were losing global and local market share to stronger competitors. What has helped them was also the fact that Japanese firms, like Mazda and Nissan, have occasionally made some radical mistakes too. Eventually, the logic of external adjustment turned out to be inevitable. The system of mass production lost against the system of flexible production, both in terms of effectiveness and ability to satisfy customer expectations. The result was the actual bankruptcy of American car companies in 2008 and the need to save them by government interventions.

The situation of the car industry is quite extreme, because the whole value chain (from construction, through technology, production and distribution to sales) is characterized by a high degree of complexity and inseparability of investments because of the large scale of operations. Once-approved solutions are very difficult to be changed, even when they stop being well adjusted to the environmental situation, because of cognitive, financial reasons and because of their internal consistency.

In less capital-consuming industries, where the value chain is less complex, adaptation of internally consistent strategies is easier as the example of Red Bull shows.[26] Today the company sales exceed

4.25 billion Euros, and it dominates in the category of energy drinks all over the world, in spite of many companies' attempts to enter this market. Dietrich Mateschitz, the founder and creator of the company's power was – as I already mentioned – a marketing director in Procter & Gamble. He first saw the drink in 1984 in Thailand, where he drank it as a highly energetic medicine to combat the inevitable affliction of globetrotters – jet lag. In exchange for a certain share in the company, he received rights to global sales and marketing of the drink from the Thai producers. The beginning was rough, as it almost always is when a new company starts with a new product. In the market of beverages completely dominated by world giants – Coca-Cola and PepsiCo – there are thousands of new products introduced every year. Almost none survives longer than a year. The reason is always the same. Each 'normal' strategy in this market requires enormous expenditure on marketing and distribution. Newly starting companies don't have enough money to invest in marketing, and distribution is very expensive and controlled by big companies. Retailers have limited shelf space and don't want to lose it by investing in new risky products. Therefore, it is almost impossible to develop a strategy coherent with requirements of this market without a lot of money and a lot of time. And the return is very unsure.

Such a situation forced Mateschitz to search for an innovative strategy model in his homeland Austria. At the beginning, when bars and night clubs treating it as a diet drink didn't want to sell Red Bull, the company addressed its offer at small retail shops and petrol stations, which were just starting to develop their product offerings. An excellent shot were night clubs where selling alcohol was forbidden, yet club-goers were still searching for the 'adrenaline' experience. Red Bull, with its high caffeine content, unidentified recipe (gossip had it, Red Bull contained amino acids and bull's intestines' in powder) and relatively high price, was just perfect for these places.[27] The company also distributed cans among students during their crazy night parties. The market and product strategy of the company has been simple and coherent from the very beginning – unusual selling points, a strange, dangerous, almost mythical product, intended exclusively for young, tough people, word of mouth, guerrilla marketing and high price. Red Bull adjusted its distribution network to this concept of sales, giving a chance to small distributors if they agreed to focus on Red Bull's exclusive distribution in a given territory. Altogether, Red Bull developed a really innovative strategy – focusing on developing a market niche and executing a low-cost strategy for an expensive product! The drink has relatively quickly attained cult status among young people in nightclubs, as well as fans of extreme sports.

Public relations was all but guaranteed by the press, who described Red Bull as an unhealthy and dangerous drink (in France it was forbidden by the French Institute of Nutrition because of the high caffeine content).

The effect was paradoxical – among its existent lovers, Red Bull became even more popular, and it expanded thanks to the market of young people searching for adventure (students!). The company further flamed their popularity by sponsoring extreme sport competitions such as snowboarding competitions, ski jumps and parachuting, as well as hang gliding and mountain canoeing. They even maintain their own teams of air acrobats in several countries. A traditional Red Bull event is Flutag – a contest, where participants design their own flying objects, which, according to the rules, must be fueled only with the power of human muscle, gravity or imagination. They jump in them from a height of 9 meters, landing in water, because none of the flying objects is actually able to stay in the air for long. The last advertising initiatives by Red Bull are the most spectacular and dangerous sports – Formula 1 and the very spectacular Red Bull Air Race – contests of acrobatic flights of small aircrafts.

In 1997 Red Bull started its expansion into the most difficult market, the US, motherland of Coca-Cola and PepsiCo, where it copied its previous marketing and distribution strategy. Characteristic vehicles with a huge Red Bull can on the roof appeared in big American cities, extreme sports were sponsored (e.g. jumps into water from high heights, hand-made car races) and TV advertising was limited to minimum. Distribution was built based on a network of small and medium distributors, from whom Red Bull required loyalty and exclusivity. In spite of the fact that in 1999, the market of energy drinks created by Red Bull in the US was relatively small (about 75 million dollars) compared to the general market of nonalcoholic beverages (about 50 billion dollars), it drew the attention of Coca-Cola and PepsiCo for two reasons. First, it was the only fast-growing (about 100% per year) segment of the stagnating market of nonalcoholic beverages (annual growth of 0.5%). Second, it was the segment with the highest margins. Red Bull defended its leading position in most of the markets, despite several new launches of new energy drinks in almost every market around the world (Monster, Rockstar, Full Throttle, KMX, Burn, Shock, No Fear, Tiger and so on) thanks to a coherent strategy of positioning its drink as far away as possible from typical products of big companies.

At the same time, it is worth noticing that Coca-Cola and Pepsi didn't fight for a position in this market fiercely, because the market itself, the product and the overall strategy and its execution programs were not coherent with their own strategies. It is difficult to imagine these companies, for which the primary customers are families, to invest in marketing and promotion underlining the wild, extreme, freaky character of their products like Red Bull has done! Red Bull has been doing this since the beginning, and its excellent web page is full of videos from strange sports sponsored by the company. Red Bull is still one step ahead of its competitors. Another unusual idea of Mateschitz was an annual Music Academy, where famous rappers, drummers, guitarists, DJs and sound engineers teach young musicians. Selection is very strict, and the academy has been visited only by a small percentage of several thousands of candidates from around the world. It is also very typical to sponsor things like Felix Baumgartner's world records breaking jump from the height of 39 km in 2012, which became the most watched event in the history of youtube.com.

Leaving aside whether Red Bull as a drink – as it promises on its web page – improves concentration, emotional state, metabolism, effectiveness and physical condition or not, the strategy of the company, worked out on a small Austrian market and consistently copied and improved upon for other markets, has certainly ensured it the position of world leader in this category. The company has gone global, starting the expansion to India and China with the same simple and coherent strategy formula – one drink, homogeneous packaging (a can or a bottle with two different volumes), exclusive distribution and sponsoring contests, sports and extreme sports events. What could be the main threat for Red Bull is obviously loss of external adjustment, but until now it has been far from it. Life speed increases, and whereas young people drink Red Bull in the morning in order to wake up, their parents drink it in the afternoon not to fall asleep. Since mass distribution networks were accepted by all social groups, Red Bull started to use them and offered mass consumers its own stands, which distinguishes the drink from the crowd of other drinks. And it has started to slightly modify its products. Within the framework of adjustment to new trends in the environment, it launched Sugarfree Red Bull, which 20 years ago would have been ridiculous. Today, it is neither ridiculous, nor does it hurt the brand. While keeping its strategy simple, consistent and coherent, Red Bull decided to adjust occasionally to changes in the environment. It added mass advertising channels, complemented its own distribution with elements of mass distribution, and minimally increased product range (the can was complemented by the bottle and a new kind of sugarfree product). The primary threat to the company's strategy, which it would be difficult to overcome, would be a radical market change toward healthy or sports beverages orientation, whose qualities would be easier to communicate and defend than in case of energy drinks.

Constant challenge

Summing up the discussion on features of a good strategy, it should be stressed again that all three features complement each other and strengthen their elementary effectiveness. When strategy is simple it is easier to reach internal consistency and external coherence. When it is coherent and simple, it is easier to communicate and implement it. That is why developing strategy is difficult, because all conditions should be met at the same time. In practice, it is rarely possible to do it in a perfect way. The most fundamental and obvious problems are natural situational contradictions, which make it difficult to guarantee strategy simplicity, and at the same time, internal consistency and good adjustment to the environment. These contradictions are almost unavoidable and demand accepting trade-offs. Sometimes company strategies are simple and consistent, but as a result of inertia, they stop being well adjusted to changing environmental conditions. An example of such strategies would be cases of local newspapers in the US and Europe, which until not long ago, had very strong market positions and very good economic results. Today, Internet technology has changed everything, taking away from newspapers both readers and revenue from advertisements. As a result, local newspapers in the US have been experiencing serious financial troubles since 2007, and the same process has begun to accelerate in Europe as well. In turn, processes of necessary internal and external adaptations aimed at maintaining strategy coherence most often complicate strategies, as organizations try to adjust to the growing number of conditions and threats.

When strategy stops being simple, its execution becomes difficult and expensive. Wal-Mart, the biggest retailer in the world, often cited as a flagship example of an extremely effective strategy, has actually only been reaching average results for many years. Its main problem might be an ever-increasing complexity of strategy of such a large company. Together with growth (Wal-Mart employees over 1.5 million people!), new types of networks (e.g. discount wholesaler Sam's Club), internationalization of activities to new markets (Asia, Europe and South America), wherein it deals with very strong local competitors, the strategy implementation becomes extremely complex. As a result, revenues grow, but margins decrease, and periodically Wal-Mart encounters spectacular strategic failures (e.g. in Germany). In a similar fashion the ultra-efficient and well-organized Foxconn faced natural problems during its internationalization drive. Following customers it expanded outside China and built its factories in the US, Central Europe and Latin America, employing over one million people in 2012. The execution of its low-cost strategy with famously detailed and centralized management style of management will be more and more difficult with growing complexity created by size and operations in different cultural and legal regimes.[28]

Maintaining simplicity and coherence is an intellectual and practical challenge, which always meets difficulties. Therefore, at any given moment, in the market there are many local, but most often not optimal (second best) strategies and but a few optimal ones, which are entirely coherent. Organizations have little influence on external events, which provoke uncertainty of success and which disturb adjustment. That is why in a complex and dynamic environment, both right key choices and achievement of external coherence is, per definition, not always possible. Simplicity and internal consistency have better-defined adversaries. They are above all managers, when they allow their organizations to drift, complicate their operations or simply don't know what their true role and responsibility in the process of developing and implementing strategy is.

7
Company Adrift – Inertia, Organizational Games and Unsure Leaders

Only leaders have the right to make key strategic choices. This is a result of their legitimization as representatives of the owners or founders of the organization, as well as from the right to take decisions given to management boards, accompanied by their accountability. Regardless of how much (and how correctly) we underline the creative and important role of an organization's participants in the development of strategy, especially in modern companies based on knowledge, the fact is that management boards, not employees, are accountable for creating strategy and final choices. Leaders can carry out this task on their own, delegate it toward lower hierarchical levels or toward a dedicated strategy team or unit. They can and should commit participants to processes of gathering information, its interpretation and formulating alternative actions. They can also come to a conclusion that strategy is not needed at all and that it is enough to control costs, keep production and sales process flexible and periodically adjust to changes that are impossible to avoid or neglect. But then again, opting for a lack of strategy is also a key choice.

The statement that the management board, or sometimes simply the CEO, is accountable for company strategy is so categorical that it deserves a better justification and arguments than just the legal and organizational ones. Research shows that leaders often lose control over companies and stop playing their role in a responsible way. Passion and discipline of strategy fades away and companies start to drift. There are three basic reasons for this, which true leaders must treat as constant challenges:

1) Organizational inertia;
2) The process of deliberate or spontaneous capturing by influential participants of a part of leaders' decision rights as well as their influence on final key choices;
3) Lack of understanding of their role in the organization by top management.

Let's look closer at each of these, one after another.

Inertia, or why companies don't adapt easily

Organizational inertia is never good or bad per se. It is a natural effect of strategic choices and an unalienable attribute of an organization's operations. Thanks to research, its main mechanisms are known, and three of them deserve particular attention: cognitive maps of top management, organizational routines and sustainable relations with the environment.[1]

The first typical driver of inertia is the process of creation and maintenance of cognitive maps of management, a theory of business world that each company management board has. In theory, this concept is called a 'mental map', a 'mental frame', a 'configuration', a 'mindset', and most often, simply a 'dominant logic'.[2] Sources of these terms are similar, because they have deep philosophical roots in questions regarding habitus – the structure of knowing and motivating. In essence, we are talking about universal mechanisms that we all use in an innate way, in most cases subconsciously, in order to explain, understand and consequently accept the world.

Managers leading a company, like other professionals, use a limited repertoire of schemes, models and solutions in order to avoid excess of information and decision alternatives. In time, based on their experience, choices and goals, they start to create certain logic of action, which in turn strengthens organizational procedures. A long time ago, this process was elegantly summarized by Winston Churchill, who said that we first shape our buildings, and afterwards our buildings shape us.

Cognitive maps define how managers perceive the world. They constitute a set of beliefs, values and filters, which play the role of navigator in a complex world full of contradictory information. They answer key strategic questions like where the company should head, who is and who is not its main competitor, who are its key customers, and so on. Cognitive maps are therefore the equivalent of normal cartographic maps – a guide in the three-dimensional business space full of turns, hills, valleys and holes. The difference between a cognitive map and a standard map is that the former usually loses its validity quicker and stops being a good guide, because the business world changes quicker than the world of Nature. In spite of this, managers have a tendency to stick to once-assumed beliefs and values, even if there are relatively strong signals of a lack of adequacy between the map and the area it depicts.[3]

There are cognitive economics in such behavior. Creation of a common cognitive map demands investment in terms of intellect and emotion. It means much discussion and agreement within the management board. Sometimes, it means imposing the boss's perspective or the perspective of the most influential member of the board. What is more, the map is strengthened by the experience of particular members from the highest level of management, as well as feedback concerning the company's financial results. The better they are, the more perfect the concept of reality will seem to members of the management board. That is why with time, within a given map, reduction of the number of cognitive categories takes places, the model of the world becomes simpler and information regarding environment and the company's operations is filtered by this model.

Based on such a map, long-term investment decisions are taken and the company's architecture is built. Rejecting or even modifying the cognitive map has important financial, organizational and social consequences, so no wonder it is treated as the last resort. As companies grow, they strengthen their pattern of action, evolve toward product and market diversification, favoring development of bureaucratic routines and concentration on achievement of consecutive sales growth at any cost (in reality or just on paper). Such declines of companies as a result of the increasing inertia of cognitive maps and patterns of behavior and actions, together with simultaneous changes of the market environment (the map no longer conforms to the area), are quite frequent in practice. The primary pattern of the company's success starts to strengthen, with time becoming its own, ineffective caricature. One of the most interesting examples of this cognitive inertia in the 20th century is the story of Polaroid, whose last remaining elements – including the brand itself – were licensed to Summit Global Group in 2009.

The company was founded in 1937 by famed inventor of polarized sunglasses, Edwin Land. In 1948, Polaroid introduced its first camera to the market, marking the beginning of a long, successful period of growth.[4] The company's history, combined with the very strong personality of its founder and longstanding president, Edwin Land, shaped the cognitive map of the company based on a range of assumptions. Managers of the company deeply believed in great, revolutionary technological projects. Growth of technology, patents, paving the way and absolute perfectionism were greatly respected values in Polaroid Corporation. A classic example of a project conducted in conformity with these norms was the S70 camera, developed by Polaroid over a period of eight years and costing over half a billion dollars in investments – during the 1960s! Another important conviction was a belief in the integrated company model, as well as control over all research and development phases and all phases of camera and film production. The third important assumption was to treat Polaroid cameras as mass products. The result of this assumption was distribution and sales in modern megastores (Wal-Mart, Target) rather than in shops specializing in photography equipment. The fourth assumption was the concept of a sales model developed some time earlier by Gillette and therefore often called the razor/blade model. The price of the camera decreased systematically in order to stimulate demand for film, which was expensive, and hence the reason Polaroid had such high margins. The last assumption was the logic behind the creators of instant photography's convictions that what customers cherished most were tangible pictures, fast: the physicality of the picture, as one of the managers has said, an 'ontological truth' of the company.[5]

This kind of cognitive map made Polaroid a global corporation and a recognizable brand. At the same time, it didn't shy away from the progress of digital imaging. Quite the contrary, as a company fueled by technological challenges, Polaroid began developing digital technology as early as the 1970s. By 1989, it controlled the best technologies, even allowing it to produce a digital camera that could take pictures with a resolution of two million pixels – obviously connected to a printer for instant printing. At the time, even the closest competitors could only offer a resolution of 0.5 million pixels. However, despite these technological possibilities, the managerial know-how and the great brand of Polaroid eventually lost the battle for the digital market. The main culprit for this was blind belief in the company's focus on the importance of the 'physicality' of the picture and the dominant financial model of inexpensive cameras and expensive films. A digital camera offered neither a tangible picture, nor film for which the producer could obtain a 70 percent margin. Their initial foray into the digital arena was regularly postponed, in spite of the fact that Polaroid had a prototype ready in 1992. At last, when it eventually appeared on the market in 1996, it had already been delayed by a couple of years, and was technically complicated and expensive. As they say, a day late and a dollar short. The sales department, though ready to cooperate with retail networks, didn't quite know what to do with a product that cost almost 1000 dollars, whereas management, in spite of some changes in its composition, didn't see the necessity of building another sales and distribution system. Since Polaroid was also used to large-scale projects and long technological and development cycles, it was unable to quickly introduce improvements and changes in its products. The company went bankrupt in 2001. Until the very end, Polaroid believed in the universal character of the razor/blade model, which had served it so well during times of the dominance of instant imaging, but which didn't make sense in the digital era.

The example of Polaroid dramatically shows how difficult it is to review the cognitive maps once set. Most often, the main trigger for such a change is a radical instability in a company – either a true crisis or a change in top management, but the example of Polaroid shows that sometimes neither the first nor the second helps. The latest financial crisis, which first and foremost affected big investment banks, has also been a good test for the inertia of cognitive maps. Cognitive maps of the management of these banks were based on many assumptions and decisions, many of which became ever more risky between 2005 and 2007. Some of them became absurd (e.g. the increase of prices of real estate will be almost eternal), other doubtful (e.g. the financial system brings additional value into the economy's functioning) and some plainly false (e.g. the market is always correctly pricing financial products). Of course, every board of management of every investment bank had its own, individual cognitive map of the market's functioning, but they were similar to one another.

Their destructive character is illustrated in the contents of an excellent book by the president of the Vanguard Mutual Fund Group, John C. Bogle: (1) Too much cost, not enough value; (2) Too much speculation, not enough investment; (3) Too much complexity, not enough simplicity;(4) Too much counting, not enough trust; (5) Too much business conduct, not enough professional conduct; (6) Too much salesmanship, not enough stewardship; (7) Too much management, not enough leadership; (8) Too much focus on things, not enough focus on commitments; (9) Too many 21st century values, not enough 18th century values; (10) Too much 'success', not enough character.[6] Each chapter in this book is devoted to one of the rules of investment banking, which was a typical element of the dominant logic shaped at the beginning of the 21st century and clearly demonstrates why these rules have become their own caricature with dangerous consequences for the whole global economy. So far, not much indicates that the global crisis and change of top management teams in practically all global investment banks have significantly changed the dominant logic of their actions.

The second typical driver of inertia (after mental maps development) is organizational routines. Routine development has been described by sociologists, economists and theorists of organization.[7] It is a natural process, neither esoteric nor complicated, a derivative of the learning process of people and organizations. This process generates knowledge, called tacit knowledge many years ago by a philosopher of science, M. Polanyi, because it is knowledge of common people, who are often unable to describe and explain it well. In practice, everyone has such knowledge – there are printing machine operators who are able to set up machines or make them print again in a stable, repetitive manner much faster than others, there are surgeons who perform standard surgeries faster and better than others, there are WRC drivers who change gears faster and take turns better than others, but many are unable to precisely explain how they do it. However, organizations cannot rely on the experimental, practical knowledge of individual members. Together with the learning process, supported by feedback information regarding the consequences of taken decisions and actions, managers try to codify practical knowledge into procedural, repetitive ways of action, or so-called explicit knowledge. I. Nonaka and H. Takeuchi underline that this is exactly how organizations build resources of knowledge needed to compete effectively: it is the so-called procedural knowledge.[8] This is exactly why organizations build routines, which are present in each company. They constitute technology of a repetitive action. They not only ensure cognitive economics (they reduce the number of information, which members of the organization must process) but they also simplify the process of problem-solving and decision-making and they accelerate their implementation.

Routines have a natural form of regulations, procedures of the 'if then' type, organizational programs (planning, making budget and assessing employees), as well as habits and rituals. Each researcher and member of the organization knows its basic dynamics – the number of routines always grows together with growth of the organization itself and its complexity. This is natural. Routines simplify, economize and accelerate actions, but also increase safety of all organization members. The other side of routines is obviously increased bureaucracy, decreased flexibility, sub-optimization, creation of a set of dominant, standard operational procedures and behaviors. The result is a growing organization's inertia.

The third mechanism of inertia is the system of sustainable relations with the environment, which each organization must build in order to be successful – from relations with suppliers to relations with distribution channels and final customers. As a result, every organization is surrounded by an ecosystem of relations with suppliers, distributors, customers and complementators, which literally amounts to hundreds or thousands of relations. Organizations become like ships, which throw many anchors at the same time and become more and more stable. However, at the same time, their possibilities of maneuvering become very limited or none. The truly problematic become the relations that initially gave the company competitive advantage (e.g. loyal distributors and retail networks selling personal computers), which, as a result of important changes in the environment, become a liability. Another example is the growing bargaining power of large retail networks, which not only dominate the market of food or domestic appliances, but also the market of construction materials (Castorama or Leroy Merlin) or cosmetics (Douglas, Sephora and Rossman). Every company wanting to build a strong position on the market must treat these networks as a main distribution channel, though the downside is that they can quite quickly start dictating the pace of innovations, the size of margins and even the marketing campaigns. In the short and medium run, any attempt to cut such relations in order to regain flexibility of strategic moves – even if it makes sense – means an instantaneous decrease in sales, possibly antagonizing influential players in the environment, an uncertain future of new distribution channels and an instantaneous reaction from competitors who overtake freed shelf space. In such cases, one must be really brave to take a decision which changes relations with the environment, if it's not just to change suppliers or hold sales to given customers. Sometimes it is simply impossible, because there are no good alternatives, and the company becomes a permanent hostage of its business environment.

As a result of its Janus-like facades, inertia constitutes one of the biggest challenges for company leaders. On one hand, it has a deep sense because it decreases risk in the life of the organization. It is also a natural fruit of the complementarity of strategic choices. Their strong mutual relations make each good strategy inertial. On the other hand, it creates an illusionary sense of safety, it decreases readiness to search for new information and experimenting, it destroys passion. The company starts repeating endlessly its own past experiences, entering the downward slope of comfort and complacency. The belief in the sustainability of the once-achieved competitive advantage starts to dominate, and awareness of the fact that on a downward slope the dominant direction is always downward disappears.

Games for power and resources

Managers act in a constant flow of events. Organization members are not an army contingent, which can be given the command to stop, stand still like during a drill, be reconfigured, and then recommence the exercise from the beginning. When managers think about strategy, particular divisions of the company must perform their tasks. They have to accept directives, produce, improve technologies, sign contracts, deliver merchandise and offer service at the same time. These flows of actions create chances for members to build their own power positions and action routines – or else to achieve control over fragments of the territories and reduce impact from the top management. In each company, there is a constant battle between members for power, impact and resources, limiting the maneuvering possibilities of the top management. Therefore, sometimes the main player becomes but a pawn on the chessboard. In this case, official strategy becomes an illusion and real impact goes to members' autonomous initiatives. It is well illustrated by the cases of three companies operating in completely different time and institutional environments.

One of the first studies well describing this phenomenon is the famous monograph of M. Crozier.[9] The most interesting of all case studies analyzed in this book concerns a group of plants called Industrial Monopoly. It is a company operating in the French state-dominated economy, fully bureaucratized and equipped with routines, which ensured the repetitiveness and predictability of its functioning. Since the process of taking decisions is centralized and the top management controls the process of creating and changing routines it seems that it enjoys full power. However, these are just appearances. As Crozier stressed, creating a totally new approach to study organizations almost 50 years ago, centralization, which became the logical consequence of such a system, makes it difficult to execute personal power. A key example of the game for power and resources in the Industrial Monopoly are the people responsible for machine setup, who, forming a kind of alliance with machine operators, start to capture real power. Machine breakdowns, frequent and natural in the production system, constitute the only important event that is impossible to formalize, and especially – as Crozier highlights – it is impossible to define whether a breakdown will happen, when it will take place and how much time is needed to really repair it. At the same time, people responsible for machine setup and repairs have practical knowledge that no other people have – making it difficult to control them. A complex game starts taking place in the plant. Leaders try to take control over breakdowns and systematically control their removal, because control of the only source of uncertainty in the world of bureaucracy gives them an important real impact and privileges.

I observed a similar phenomenon many years ago carrying out research over cooperation between special research units and industrial companies in the process of creating and implementing industrial technical innovations in Poland at the end of the1970s.[10] In the centralized socialist economy, innovations constituted one of the main sources of uncertainty – a process that could not be well planned and controlled in spite of all institutional attempts. Organizational units, subordinate to industrial ministries (coordinating units), conducted a refined game regarding the development and implementation of technological innovations, in order to prevent routinization of this process and to capture control of resources and actions from decision-makers. The game had three principal rules.

The first consisted of creating an atmosphere of a great opportunity and a great media event around innovation development. The objective was to make it virtually impossible to evaluate such a case using typical financial or organizational rules. R&D units and industrial companies committed to this process used completely modern (or maybe always existing) methods. They actively used the language of contemporary politics, wrapping the given initiative in key political wording and leveraging Communist Party political, social and economic lingo. They involved media, sought allies in order to extend the platform of communication and tenders, they promoted innovators as heroes, they actively fought for additional means and for giving the whole process a status of an exceptional undertaking that cannot be subjected to normal routines and plans. Members of this process very effectively used relationships and different organizational and/or any political roles they played (today we would call it "social capital" of managers), in order to reach as high as possible across the hierarchy of decision-makers and convince them of the political and economic importance of the particular technological innovation.

The second rule, which complemented the first, concerned institutional cooperation within industrial ministries and business associations. Objectives of new ventures were formulated generally enough not to face a decisive opposition and not to create conflicts. Cooperating units protected access to important and specific information from the supervisory bodies and tried to execute the whole innovation implementation process in small and partially camouflaged strategic moves, gradually and flexibly formulating the final shape of the undertaking. Particular decisions and actions were taken by various cooperating actors involved in the process, and their limited utilization of resources allowed avoidance of the necessity to obtain approval of decision-makers from the highest level of the hierarchy. Some important, but partial, decisions were moved to the highest levels of hierarchy, and after approval, became an element of the process-building escalating commitment, from which it was difficult to withdraw later. In such a way, the process became blurred and therefore nontransparent for decision-makers of the higher level in the organization's hierarchy, thereby reducing their ability to influence the form, content and outcome of the game.

The third rule was especially interesting. The innovation process usually created conflicts that could reveal real intentions of the players and ways they bypass formal plans and procedures for resource allocation. In order to prevent early exposure of the unplanned actions and resource allocation, involved parties always searched for external arbiters of conflicts. Sources of potential conflicts in such atypically realized processes were varied, so were their content and form. In order to not build organizational routines for conflict solving, actors of the process each time sought an arbiter, a peacemaker, who could impose compromising solutions for a precise problem or situation. Thanks to this, the conflict didn't change the balance of powers (each conflict was considered separately and with an appropriate technical, economic and organizational justification) and remained an inter-organizational conflict. Feelings, emotions, positions of particular persons remained practically unthreatened, which decreased the probability of escalating conflicts.

By applying this set of rules, both R&D and industrial units, formally subordinated to the central ministries power and central planning logic, obtained quite an autonomy of action in practice. They overtook real decision competences and received additional means and resources for their undertakings, well beyond formal plans allocation. In an apparently strict hierarchical and centrally managed political and economic system, with a petrified structure of dependences, technical innovations constituted the source of uncertainty, which, because of the lack of routines and repetitiveness, became a springboard for the game for power, impact and attention of decision-makers of the highest levels.

It is absolutely extraordinary that over 20 years later a very similar process, only this time in the company Intel, an organization with an exemplary practices of strategic management, is described by its former president A. S. Grove together with a scientist from Stanford, R. Burgelman. The point of departure of the authors is the analysis of real expenditure related to research and development on the planned (in conformity with the approved strategy of Intel) and autonomous initiatives, understood as projects realized by the middle management and in a limited way conforming to the approved budgets. According to the authors' assessment, between 1976 and 2005, autonomous expenditures made up 13 to 50 percent of the total means of research and development! One of the classic examples was the project of microprocessors based on RISC (Reduced Instruction Set Computing) architecture, described by authors as follows:

In the late 1980s, Intel's official corporate strategy had been not to enter the RISC business, but rather to focus its induced strategy process on its x86 (CISC) architecture. The sole-source strategy for the 386 processor was highly successful, and with the upcoming 486 microprocessor, Intel was poised to further strengthen its position as the architectural leader in the early 1990s. Intel top management called RISC 'the technology of the have not.' Operating autonomously, however, a young engineer had been attempting to get Intel into the RISC processor business ever since joining the company in 1982. He ventured to sell the design for the i860 processor to top management as a co-processor for the 486 rather than as a stand-alone processor. By the time top management realized what their 'co-processor' was, he and two other champions had already lined up a workstation customer base that was different from the companies who purchased the 486 chips. Thus, the i860 team could argue that they were broadening Intel's business rather than cannibalizing it. Even though top management had not officially sanctioned its development, Intel did, in fact, introduce the i860 as a stand-alone RISC microprocessor in February 1989. At the time, a top-level executive pointed out that RISC was still viewed as relatively less important than CISC in Intel's strategy, but that its availability made it possible for Intel to be a strong competitor in what might become an important new market.

The threat of RISC, however, took a different form than envisaged by the RISC supporters within Intel. Some industry observers interpreted the introduction of the i860 as a signal that Intel was endorsing RISC. But this could confuse Intel's existing PC OEM customers, who might fear that Intel would reduce support for the x86 architecture in the future. That fear was not unfounded. The RISC team within Intel had created a strong following. Distinct CISC and RISC camps had formed and they were competing for the best engineering talent of the company. The RISC effort siphoned off hundreds of people just on the marketing side. By 1989, RISC-based processor development had begun to absorb about one third of the total resources allocated to microprocessor development. The two camps were also trying to gain allies in the industry (Microsoft encouraged the i860; Compaq opposed it). The battle between CISC and RISC within Intel had turned into 'civil war.' RISC proponents prepared a development trajectory showing the Intel architecture transitioning to RISC after the 486 and wanted to rename the i860 processor 486r to facilitate the transition. But in response to serious concerns by Intel's vice president of marketing and other senior executives, top management decided that the i860 could not be renamed 486r. Eventually, the i860 was not successful because demand for it petered out as every workstation vendor decided to develop its own RISC processor. By 1993, most of the technical people from the i860 team had left Intel. Intel, however, succeeded in retaining many members of the team who had honed skills in ecosystem development. Looking back, this was a confusing period for Intel. The i860 was a very successful renegade product that could have destroyed the virtuous circle enjoyed by the Intel architecture.[11]

If not for the fact that the whole story was cited by the former CEO of the company, it would sound incredible. We deal with the company that is a benchmark of management for companies around the world. We deal with a global leader of the market of microprocessors. The company's strategy is developed based on a technological concept, which becomes market winner. And simultaneously, within the effectively managed company a group of renegades – acting against the strategy and will of the board of management – involves a large team of people, as well as external organizations, in a project going against the official strategy and ties one-third of the giant research and development expenditures to this project! Grove and Burgelman, discussing events from that period, say that if we were supposed to seek a positive interpretation, you can say that the board of management decided to play the role of a referee who waits to see which of the technological camps in the company wins. A negative interpretation is reactive, defensive behavior of the board of management. It was simply a chaos, which no one really controlled. And they conclude: 'And so it was.'[12]

As one can see, the type of environment, economy and company doesn't change much in this respect. Managers and employees of lower levels are able to use sources of uncertainty in the company to overtake control over events and resources. Management boards think that they manage companies, but they actually become almost passive observers of decisions and events – until they recover and regain control and/or eliminate via routines consecutive sources of uncertainty. The price, which they must pay for routinization is, as Crozier noticed, another loss of control. And thanks to that, the games for power and resources in a company are endless, deforming and modifying their strategies in action.

Unsure leaders

When, in October 2004, A. G. Lafley took the position of CEO of Procter & Gamble, the world leader on the market of consumer products from food to cosmetics, he had two problems. First, it was his debut as the president of the management board in a company with such a large scale of operations. Second, P&G was in trouble. The program of radical restructuring announced at the end of the 1990s called *Organization 2005* wasn't successful. A. G. Lafley started his mandate in an unusual way – from a seminar, to which he invited other managers, consultants and ... the old 95-year-old guru in the field of management, Peter Drucker. The seminar covered simple questions, ones that have fundamental consequences and are asked by far too seldom in theory and practice: What is the role of a company president? Do they have their own unique tasks? What are their unique tasks, that is, tasks which only they should perform and which only they must perform? Since Peter Drucker is no longer alive, let's give the floor to Lafley: 'He argued that people wrongly view CEOs as coaches and utility infielders who jump in to solve problems as needed, and that CEOs indeed have work that is their own.' In 2004 Drucker said, 'The CEO is the link between the Inside that is "the organization", and the Outside of society, economy, technology, markets, and customers. Inside there are only *costs*. *Results* are only on the outside.'[13]

Before we address the question regarding the role of companies' leaders, let's think for a while about why in the 21st century, in one of the largest American corporations, which is almost a Mecca for management theorists and practitioners, the new CEO asks the question: 'what does my work consist of?' The problem, which Lafley understood better than other CEOs of many companies, is that the world of researchers, consultants and practitioners is divided into two almost separate groups with diverse opinions regarding the role of the companies' leaders.[14] One group states that leaders (in the old-fashioned meaning of this word, this is members of the board of management and the CEO of the company) are a key asset of the company, and they noticeably distinguish the managerial roles from leadership roles. Managers make order of the company's functioning, but without a real leader – exercising his or her unique role – organizations are condemned to mediocrity. Therefore, supporters of this view are mainly interested in what the principal tasks of company leaders are, how they can effectively play the role of a link between the environment and the company, motivate subordinates to extraordinary achievements and entrepreneurial behaviors, reaching out of standard procedures and routines. As J. P. Kotter, one of the gurus of this group, stated in a classic article on the role of leaders, the latter don't plan, don't solve problems, don't even organize work of other people. The true role of leaders is to prepare the organization for changes and deal with them.[15]

The second (smaller, but also competent) group of thinkers claims that the role and importance of leaders are exaggerated or even fictitious, because in reality, research doesn't show any important relation between the company's effectiveness and the actions of its leaders, and the rich literature in the field of leadership constitutes another example of mass demand for heroes. As these researchers stress, more often than not, employees learn about the vision and the strategy from corporate leaflets, CDs or Intranet. They treat it as a PR exercise, and strategy is less important for them than standard operational procedures. In the meantime, the leader himself or herself, is very busy giving interviews, attending TV programs, displaying presentations at endless conferences for stakeholders, and has a very vague idea about what is actually going on in the company. Of course, there is some mean underlining in such a description of behaviors of many leaders. What's more, the above mentioned research on the role of inertia and organizational games show real limitations of the executive power of leaders. That's why the dispute over the importance of leaders in the company is serious – both theoretically and practically. Unfortunately, it often omits the fundamental distinction between normative expectations from the company's leader (what his/her role should be – and that is what the first group of researchers is interested in) and the description of behaviors of many quasi-leaders in reality (what they actually do – and this is what the other group is interested in). What is interesting for us here is the normative role of the leader as the top strategist of the company, that is, the exact questions Lafley posed.

Hundreds or thousands of books have been written on this topic. The prestigious journal for managers, the 'Harvard Business Review', has devoted entire issues to the problem of leadership. At the best international business schools, courses in leadership are the most sought-after, and in the worn-out world of meanings and endless recipes, managers have recently been advised to seek inspiration in literature. Maybe presidents and managers of companies should read Dostoyevsky, Tolstoy, Shakespeare, Machiavelli, Clausewitz or Sun Tzu in the search for the essence of leadership and their roles. I recommend to company leaders a famous Polish sci-fi writer and a great philosopher, Stanislaw Lem. He is best known for his novel, *Solaris* (a third movie based on this novel featured in 2002 George Clooney and Natascha McElhone), but the issue of leadership is addressed in detail in his classic sci-fi novel *The Invincible*.[16] There is one scene in this book that dramatically illustrates the true role of the leader – in this case a commander of a spaceship under attack.

The space cruiser *Invincible*, which has landed on the planet Regis III, sends an 80-ton self-propelled and armed in every possible weapon war vehicle called Cyclope on a reconnaissance mission to assess potential threats. The machine eventually gets reprogrammed by an enemy and attacks its own spaceship. Horpach, the captain of the spaceship, decides to fight against his own strongest military unit. In the commander room of the spaceship, the following short dialog takes place[17]:

> – *I need full thrust – said Horpach without taking his eyes off the screen. The chief engineer's fingers struck full chords on the control keyboard as if he was playing a piano.*

– Full power in six minutes – he replied.

– I need full thrust – Horpach repeated in the same tone of voice and there was such an absolute silence in the room that you could hear relays buzz behind enameled compartments, as if a beehive was waking up out there.

– 'The reactor casing is too cold,' the Chief Engineer started, and then Horpach turned around and facing him directly, repeated for the third time in the same steady, unchanged voice:

– I need FULL power.

Without a word the chief engineer lifted his hand toward the master switch. Alarm signals bleated in staccato bursts throughout the spaceship, and the running men's steps followed like a distant roll of drums as they hurried to the battle stations. Horpach glanced at the video screen again. Nobody said a word, but everyone understood by now that the impossible was about to happen: the commander was preparing to go into battle with his own Cyclope.

Those who have read the novel know the rest. The commander hits Cyclope with enough power to boil a small sea and destroys it. Only later, he admits straightforwardly to his deputy that he didn't know what to do. But he analyzed the situation, interpreted the threat and decided how to react to it.

There are almost all threads necessary to understand the essence of leadership there. There is the formal role of the spaceship's commander. There is a situation of threat, which requires immediate interpretation and action. There is a sense of uncertainty, lack of time and possibility to gather enough information in order to take an optimal decision. There are rational behaviors of subordinates that do not fit at all into the situation's drama. And finally, there are everyone's eyes looking at the leader, with a strong expectation that he knows more and better.

Often the leader doesn't know more and better, but she or he should be able to interpret the situation in the organization's environment and take a decision. He is accountable for the company's reaction to the situation in the environment and the final results. The leader who doesn't accept it, doesn't understand his/her basic role in the company. Managers and employees are responsible for every concrete action and activity. Leaders are responsible for making sense of events in the environment and translating them into required reactions of the organization. They must have the courage to use judgment informed by experience and analysis and take executive decisions, even if they don't know exactly what to do, because their true role in the process of developing company strategy is to create a comfort zone for competent subordinates. It is not about feeling that the company is better and smarter than competitors. The essence of the comfort zone, which the leader must create, is the feeling that we have passions and dreams, we know what the general trends and tendencies in the environment are, and we know where we are going to and what we should do. And that we can make it. No other person can more effectively create this kind of comfort zone than the company's leaders. That's why without leaders, there is no passion and discipline of strategy.

Notes

1 What Is Strategy Anyway?

1. Sun-tzu (1994) *The Art of War* (translation by R. D. Sawyer), New York: Barnes & Noble Book; M. Musahi (1974) *A Book of Five Rings* (translation by V. Harris), London: Allison and Busby; T. von Ghyczy, B.von Oetinger and Ch. Basford (2001) *Clausewitz on Strategy*, New York: Wiley; M. Porter (1980) *Competitive Strategy*, New York: The Free Press.
2. L. Gratton (2007) *Hot Spots: Why Some Teams, Workplaces, and Organisations Buzz with Energy – and Others Don't*, Harlow: Prentice Hall, p. 1.
3. A. Canato and A. Giangreco (2011) 'Gurus or Wizards? A Review of the Role of Management Consultants', *European Management Review*, 8, 231–44.
4. W. Ch. Kim and R. Mauborgne (2005) *Blue Ocean Strategy*, Boston: Harvard Business School Press.
5. R. Rumelt, D. E. Schendel and D. J. Teece (1994) *Fundamental Issues in Strategy: A Research Agenda*, Boston: Harvard Business School Press.
6. S. Cummings and W. Daellenbach (2008) 'A Guide to the Future of Strategy? The History of Long Range Planning', *Long Range Planning*, 43, 234–63.
7. G. Kolotko (2011) *Truth, Errors and Lies: Politics and Economics in a Volatile World*, New York: Columbia University Press.
8. Ch. Kobrak (2013) 'Concluding Thoughts on the Use and Abuse of Financial History: Panics and Public Policy', in Ch. Kobrak and M. Wilkins (eds) *History and Financial Crisis: Lessons from the 20th Century*, Abingdon: Routledge; Ch. Kobrak and M. Wilkins (2011) 'The "2008 Crisis" in an Economic History Perspective: Looking at the Twentieth Century', *Business History*, 53, 175–92.
9. R. P. Rumelt (2009) 'Strategy in a "Structural Break" ', *The McKinsey Quarterly*, 1, 35. See also recent book by R. Rumelt (2011) *Good Strategy, Bad Strategy: The Difference and Why it Matters*, London: Profile Books.

2 Passion and Strategic Choices

1. M. Cardon, J. Wincent, J. Singh and M. Drnovsek (2009) 'The Nature and Experience of Entrepreneurial Passion', *Academy of Management Review*, 34, 511–32.
2. http://knowledge.wharton.upenn.edu/india/article.cfm?articleid=4414, accessed November 20, 2009.
3. M. Weber (1919) *Politik als Beruf, Wissenschaft als Beruf*, Berlin: Duncker and Humblot: as cited in P. Landri (2007) 'The Pragmatics of Passion: A Sociology of Attachment to Mathematics', *Organization*, 14, 417.
4. M. Cardon, J. Wincent, J. Singh and M. Drnovsek (2009) 'The Nature and Experience of Entrepreneurial Passion', *Academy of Management Review*, 34, 511–32.

5. W. Isaacson (2011) *Steve Jobs*, New York: Simon Schuster.
6. The fate of Nokia, which until the late 1990s was a prime example of innovative and fast strategy, shows how quickly the status of a great and innovative company can change. See for example Y. Doz and M. Kosonen (2008) *Fast Strategy: How Strategic Agility Will Help You Stay Ahead of the Game*, Edinburgh: Pearson Education.
7. J. P. Womack, D. T. Jones and D. Ross (1990) *The Machine That Changed the World*, New York: Harper.
8. A. Farhoomand, H. Joshi and Samuel Tsang (2009) *Nintendo's Disruptive Strategy*, Asia Case Research Center, Hong Kong: The University of Hong Kong.
9. M. Yunus (2008) *Building Social Business: The New Kind of Capitalism That Serves Humanity's Most Pressing Needs*, New York: Public Affairs.
10. A. Farhoomand, H.Joshi and S. Tsang (2009) *Nintendo's Disruptive Strategy*, Asia Case Research Center, Hong Kong: The University of Hong Kong.
11. D. Kahneman (2012) *Thinking, Fast and Slow*, London: Penguin Books; Dane, E. and Pratt, M. (2007) 'Exploring Intuition and its Role in Managerial Decision Making', *Academy of Management Review*, 32, 33–54.
12. M. Gladwell (2008) *Outliers: The Story of Success*, New York: Little, Brown and Company.
13. D. Kahneman (2012) *Thinking, Fast and Slow*, London: Penguin Books, p. 240.
14. T. Felin and R. R. Zenger (2009) 'Entrepreneurs as Theorists: On the Origins of Collective Beliefs and Novel Strategies', *Strategic Entrepreneurship Journal*, 3, 127–46; E. Dane and M. Pratt (2007) 'Exploring Intuition and its Role in Managerial Decision Making', *Academy of Management Review*, 32, 33–54; J. H. Dyer, H. B. Gregersen and C. M. Christensen (2009) 'The Innovator's DNA', *Harvard Business Review*, December.
15. A. Mayo and N. Noria (2005) *In Their Time: The Greatest Business Leaders of the Twentieth Century*, Boston: Harvard Business School Press.
16. E. Dane and M. Pratt (2007),'Exploring Intuition and Its Role in Managerial Decision Making', *Academy of Management Review*, 32, 43.
17. G. L. Ge and D. Z. Ding (2008) 'A Strategic Analysis of Surfing Chinese Manufacturers: The Case of Galanz', *Asian Pacific Journal of Management*, 25, 667–83.
18. M. Kostera (2012) *Archetypes and Organizations*, Cheltenham: Edward Elgar.
19. http://knowledge.wharton.upenn.edu/india/article.cfm?articleid=4413, accessed December 16, 2012.
20. This idea comes from the book by J. Ridderstrale and K. Nordstrom (2000) *Funky Business: Talent Makes Capital Dance*, London: Pearson Education.
21. J. H. Freemen and M. T. Hannan (1989) *Organizational Ecology*, Boston: Harvard University Press, Cambridge; P. Ghewamat (1991) *Commitment*, New York: The Free Press.
22. The processes of lock-in and lock-out are discussed by P. Ghewamat (1991) *Commitment*, New York: The Free Press, Chapter 2. See also an insightful analysis of interrelated choices in J. Roberts (2004) *The Modern Firm*, Oxford: Oxford University Press.
23. D. Miller (1990) *The Icarus Paradox: How Exceptional Companies Bring About Their Own Downfall*, New York: Harper Business.
24. E. Baraldi (2008) 'Strategy in Industrial Networks: Experiences from IKEA', *California Management Review*, 50 (4), 99–126; D. Hambrick and

J. W. Fredrickson (2005) 'Are you Sure you have a Strategy?' *Academy of Management Executive* 19, 51–62; R. Normann and R. Ramirez (1993) 'From Value Chain to Value Constellation: Designing Interactive Strategy', *Harvard Business Review*, July/August, 65–77.
25. T. Moon (2004) *IKEA Invades America*, HBS case study 9-504-094.

3   Discipline of Strategy Execution: Sensemaking and Territory

1. D. Goleman, R. E. Boyatzis, A. McKee (2004) *Primal Leadership: Learning to Lead with Emotional Intelligence*, Boston: Harvard Business School Press.
2. C. M. Christensen (1997) *The Innovator's Dilemma*, Boston: Harvard Business School Press.
3. G. Hamel and B. Breen (2007) *The Future of Management*, Boston: Harvard Business Press; R. M. Grant (2008) 'The Future of Management: Where Is Gary Hamel Leading us', *Long Range Planning*, 41, 478.
4. P. Saffo (2007) 'Six Rules for Accurate Effective Forecasting', *Harvard Business Review*, July–August, 130.
5. D. N. Sull and M. Escobari (2004) *Success against the Odds*, Oxford: Elsevier/Campus Press, Chapter 3.
6. D. A. Levinthal and J. G. March (1993) 'The myopia of learning', *Strategic Management Journal*, 14, 95–112; B. K. Boyd and J. Fulk (1996) 'Executive scanning and perceived uncertainty: A multidimensional model', *Journal of Management*, 22, 1–21.
7. D. N. Sull (2005) 'Strategy as Active Waiting', *Harvard Business Review*, September, 121–9.
8. https://www.deloitte.com/view/en_GX/global/industries/technology-media-telecommunications/deloitte-technology-fast-500, accessed January 19, 2013.
9. M. E. Raynor (2007) *The Strategy Paradox*, New York: Doubleday.
10. M. E. Raynor (2007) *The Strategy Paradox*, New York: Doubleday.
11. J. Bower (1994) *Jack Welch: General Electric's Revolutionary*, HBS case study 9-394-065; J. Welch and S. Welch (2006) *Winning*, New York: HarperBusiness.
12. D. Sull and M. Escobari (2004) *Success against the Odds*, Oxford: Elsevier/Campus Press, Chapter 3.
13. P. Kotler (2004) *Kotler on Marketing*, New York: The Free Press.
14. D.J. Collis and M. G. Rukstad (2008) 'Can You Say What Your Strategy Is?' *Harvard Business Review*, April, 82–90.
15. M. Skapinker (2000) 'A Lesson in Small-Town Economics', *Financial Times*, November 30, p. 11; C. Markides (2000) *All the Right Moves*, Boston: Harvard Business School Press, Chapter 1; C. Markides (1999) 'Strategy as Making Choices: A Discussion with John Bachmann, Managing Principal of Edward Jones', *European Management Journal*, 17, 275–85.
16. www.edwardjones.com, accessed December 24, 2012.
17. W. Issacson (2011) *Steve Jobs*, New York: Simon&Schuster, Chapter 30.
18. Personal interviews of the author in China.
19. Personal interviews with founders of the company.

20. A. G. Lafley (2009) 'What Only the CEO Can Do', *Harvard Business Review*, May, p. 60.
21. J. Roberts (2004) *The Modern Firm*, Oxford: Oxford University Press.
22. M. W. Johnson (2010) *Seizing the White Space: Business Model Innovation for Growth and Renewal*, Boston: Harvard Business Press.

4   Discipline of Strategy Execution: Goals and Business Model

1. M. Friedman (1970) 'The Social Responsibility of Business Is to Increase its Profits', *The New York Times Magazine*, September 13.
2. S. Rangan and T. Obloj (2009) *Corporate Global Citizenship: A Strategy Perspective on What and How*, INSEAD: Fontainebleau.
3. K. Obloj and S. Cavaleri (1993) *Management Systems: A Global Perspective*, Belmont: Wadsworth.
4. An echo of these classical ideas developed by systems and cybernetics thinkers like L. von Bertalanffy, W. R. Ashby, C. W. Churchman, S. Beer, C. B. Checkland, J. D. Steinbruner is very visible in the concept of Balanced Score-card that became a very popular way to operationalize goal setting, especially in larger firms. See R. S. Norton and D. P. Kaplan (1996) *Balanced Scorecard*, Boston: Harvard Business School Press.
5. R. Cyert and J. G. March (1963) *The Behavioral Theory of the Firm*, Englewood Cliffs: Prentice-Hall.
6. H. A. Simon (1964) 'On the Concept of Organizational Goal', *Administrative Science Quarterly*, 9, 1–22.
7. R. S. Norton and D. P. Kaplan (1996) *Balanced Scorecard*, Boston: Harvard Business School Press.
8. Interview with M. O'Leary, *The Wall Street Journal*, December 9, 2009, 12.
9. G. L. Ge and D. Z. Ding (2008) 'A Strategic Analysis of Surfing Chinese Manufacturers: The Case of Galanz', *Asian Pacific Journal of Management*, 25, 667–83.
10. J. Collins (2001) *Good to Great*, New York: William Collins.
11. G. Hamel and C. K. Prahalad (1994) *Competing for the Future*, Boston: Harvard Business School Press.
12. J. Collins and J. I. Porras (2004) *Build to Last: Successful Habits of Visionary Companies*, New York: HarperBusiness.
13. T. Obloj, K. Obloj and M. Pratt (2010) 'Dominant Logic and Entrepreneurial Firms Performance in a Transitional Market', *Entrepreneurship: Theory and Practice*, 34, 151–70; M. Kostera and K. Obłoj (2010) 'Archetypes of Rivalry: Narrative Responses of Polish Radio Station Managers to Perceived Environmental Change', *Journal of Organizational Change Management*, 23, 564–77.
14. M. E. Raynor (2007) *The Strategy Paradox*, New York: Doubleday.
15. L. Bossidy and R. Charan (2002) *Execution: The Discipline of Getting Things Done*, New York: Crown Business, 226.
16. R. Charan (2007) *Know-How: The 8 Skills That Separate People Who Perform from Those Who Don't*, New York: Crown Business, 198.

17. C. A. Bartlett and M. Wozny (2005) *GE's Two-Decade Transformation: Jack Welch's Leadership*, Harvard Business School case study 9-399-150; K. Obloj, D. Cushman, A. K. Kozminski (1995) *Winning: A Continuous Improvement Theory in High Performing Organizations*, Albany: SUNY Press.
18. K. Obloj and M. Pratt (2005) 'Happy Kids and Mature Losers: Differentiating the Dominant Logics of Successful and Unsuccessful Firms in Emerging Markets' in R. Bettis' (ed.) *Strategy in Transition*, Oxford: Blackwell.
19. R. Amit and P. J. Schoemaker (1993) 'Strategic Assets and Organizational Rent', *Strategic Management Journal*, 14, 33–46.
20. K. Obloj and T. Obloj (2006) 'Diminishing Returns from Reputation: Do Followers Have a Competitive Advantage?', *Corporate Reputation Review*, 9, 213–24.
21. T. S. Stewart (2001) 'Accounting Gets Radical', *Fortune*, April 16.
22. See C. K. Prahalad and G. Hamel (1990) 'The Core Competence of the Corporation', *Harvard Business Review*, May-June, 79–91; G. Hamel (2000) *Strategy as Revolution*, Boston: Harvard Business School Press; K. M. Eisenhardt and J. M. Martin (2000) 'Dynamic Capabilities: What Are they', *Strategic Management Journal*, 21, 1105–21. The term 'core competence' is used more commonly in consulting and managerial practice; dynamic capabilities are more often used in theoretical analysis and writing.
23. Company annual report (2008).
24. S. Tully (1999) 'Watch Out! Here Comes Crocodile Claude', *Fortune*, December 20.
25. K. M. Eisenhardt and D. N. Sull (2001) 'Strategy as Simple Rules', *Harvard Business Review*, January, 107–16.
26. The term was coined by M. Porter (1985) *Competitive Advantage*, New York: Free Press.
27. K. Werbach (2000) 'Syndication: The Emerging Model for Business in the Internet Era', *Harvard Business Review*, May–June, 84–93.
28. B. Iyer and T. Davenport (2008) 'Reverse Engineering Google's Innovation Machine', *Harvard Business Review*, April, 58–68.
29. http://www.thisisnoble.com/index.php?option=com_content&view=article&id=637&Itemid=471, accessed December 1, 2009.
30. Ch. Handy (1990) *The Age of Unreason*, Boston: Harvard Business School Press, Chapter. 4.
31. 'Outsourcing to India' (2001) *Economist*, May 5–1, 69–72.
32. S. N. Mehta (2001) 'Cisco Fractures Its Own Fairy Tale', *Fortune*, May 14; E. Luce and I. L. Kehoe (2001) 'Cisco's New Economy', *Financial Times*, April 4 23 and April 5, 21.
33. B. Worthen and J. Scheck (2009) 'As Growth Slows, Ex-Allies Square Off in a Tech Turf War', *Wall Street Journal*, March 17, 16–17.
34. 'HP Deal Intensifies Rivalry with Cisco', *International Herald Tribune*, November 13, 2009, 18.

5   The Effect of Passion and Discipline – Competitive Advantage

1. See P. Drucker (1964) *Managing for Results*, New York: HarperCollins; K. R. Andrews (1971) *The Concept of Corporate Strategy*, Homewood: Irwin;

K. Ohmae (1982) *The Mind of the Strategist*, New York: McGraw-Hill; M. Porter (1980) *Competitive Advantage*, New York: The Free Press; G. Hamel and C. K. Prahalad (1994) *Competing for the Future*, Boston: Harvard Business Press; R. Rumelt, D. E. Schendel and D. J. Teece (1995) *Fundamental Issues in Strategy: A Research Agenda*, Boston: Harvard Business School Press; A. J. Slywotzky (1995) *Value Migration: How to Think Several Moves Ahead of Competition*, Boston: Harvard Business School Press; W. Ch. Kim and R. Mauborgne (2005) *Blue Ocean Strategy*, Boston: Harvard Business School Press.

2. M. Porter (1980) *Competitive Strategy*, New York: The Free Press.

3. The literature of resource-based view is extremely rich and has been growing for last 20 years. See J. Barney (1991) 'Resources and Sustained Competitive Advantage', *Journal of Management*, 17, 99–120; J. T. Mahoney and J. Pandian (1992) 'The Resource-Based View in the Conversation of Strategic Management', *Strategic Management Journal*, 13, 363–80; K.Obloj and P. Joynt (1992) Rethinking Strategic Management, Bodo Graduate Business School Working Paper 9095; D. Teece, G. Pisano and A. Shuen (1997) 'Dynamic Capabilities and Strategic Management', *Strategic Management Journal*, 18, 509–33; J. Barney (2001) 'Is the Resource-Based "View" a Useful Perspective for Strategic Management Research? Yes', *Academy of Management Review*, 26, 41–56; S. L. Newbert (2007) 'Empirical Research on the Resource-Based View of the Firm: Assessment and Suggestions for Future Research', *Strategic Management Journal*, 28, 121–46.

4. K. M. Eisenhardt and J. M. Martin (2000) 'Dynamic Capabilities: What Are They?', *Strategic Management Journal*, 21, 1105–21.

5. S. A. Lippman and R. P. Rumelt (1982) 'Uncertain Imitability: An Analysis of Inter Firm Differences in Efficiency under Competition', *The Bell Journal of Economics*, 13, 418–38; I. Dierickx, K. Cool (1989) 'Asset Stock Accumulation and Sustainability of Competitive Advantage', *Management Science*, 35, 1504–13.

6. T. Powell (2001) 'Competitive Advantage: Logical and Philosophical Considerations', *Strategic Management Journal*, 22, 875–88.

7. G. Ray, J. Barney and W. Muhanna (2004) 'Capabilities, Business Processes, and Competitive Advantage: Choosing the Dependent Variable in Empirical Tests of the Resource-Based View', *Strategic Management Journal*, 25, 23–37.

8. See discussion in S. L. Newbert (2007) 'Empirical Research on the Resource-Based View of the Firm: Assessment and Suggestions for Future Research', *Strategic Management Journal*, 28, 121–46.

9. G. Ray, J. Barney and W. Muhanna (2004) 'Capabilities, Business Processes, and Competitive Advantage: Choosing the Dependent Variable in Empirical Tests of the Resource-Based View', *Strategic Management Journal*, 25, 23–37.

10. T. Powell (2001) 'Competitive Advantage: Logical and Philosophical Considerations', *Strategic Management Journal*, 22, 885.

11. There are many typologies of competitive advantage. This one combines approaches of M. Porter (1980) *Competitive Strategy*, New York: The Free Press; K. Ohmae (1982) *The Mind of the Strategist*, New York: McGraw-Hill; M. Petraff (1993) 'The Cornerstones of Competitive Advantage: A Resource-Based View', *Strategic Management Journal*, 14, 179–91.

12. D. Henderson (1974) *The Experience Curve Revisited* in C. W. Stern, G. Stalk (eds) *Perspectives on Strategy*, New York: Wiley.

13. A. Sloan (1990) *My Years with General Motors*, New York: Crown Business (reissue edition).
14. M. Treacy and F. Wiersema (1995) *The Discipline of Market Leaders*, New York: Addison-Wesley; C. Shapiro and H. A. Variana (1999) *Information Rules*, Boston: Harvard Business School Press.
15. V. Shankar (2001) 'Segmentation: Making Sure the Customer Fits', Mastering Management Series 15, *Financial Times*, January 22.
16. The German companies that followed these strategies were named 'hidden champions'. See H. Simon (2009) *Hidden Champions of the Twenty-First Century*, London: Springer and H. Simon (1996) *Hidden Champions: Lessons from 500 of the World's Best Unknown Companies*, Boston: Harvard Business School Press.
17. A. M. Brandenburger and B. J. Nalebuff (1995) 'The Right Game: Use Game Theory to Shape Strategy', *Harvard Business Review*, July–August, 57–71.
18. A. A. Ullman (1996) *The Swatch in 1993* in P. Wright, M. J. Kroll and J. Parnell (eds) *Strategic Management*, Englewood Cliffs: Prentice Hall, 374.
19. http://en.wikipedia.org/wiki/Swatch, accessed December 20, 2012.
20. *South China Morning Post*, Watches & Timepieces section, November 13, 2009.
21. L. Carroll (2011) *Through the Looking Glass*, London: Penguin Group (The original citation from Chapter 2 (p. 46) is as follows: 'it takes all the running you can do to stay in the same place').
22. W. P. Burnett and M. T. Hansen (1996) 'The Red Queen of Organizational Evolution', *Strategic Management Journal*, 17, 139–57.
23. M. Porter (1980) *Competitive Strategy*, New York: The Free Press.
24. I introduced this distinction in K. Obloj, D. Cushman and A. K. Kozminski (1995) *Winning: Continuous Improvement Theory in High-Performance Organizations*, Albany: SUNY Press, Chapter 7.
25. J. Barney (1991) 'Resources and Sustained Competitive Advantage', *Journal of Management*, 17, 99–120.

6   What Makes a Good Strategy?

1. O. Solvell and M. E. Porter (2008) *Finland and Nokia: Creating the World's Most Competitive Economy*, Harvard Business School case study 9-702-427; J. Roberts (2004) *The Modern Firm*, Oxford: Oxford University Press, 274–80; Y. Doz and M. Kosonen (2008) *Fast Strategy: How Strategic Agility Will Help You Stay Ahead of the Game*, Edinburgh: Pearson Education.
2. 'Bears at the Door', *Economist*, January 15, 2010, 57.
3. D. J. Collis and M. G. Rukstad (2008) 'Can You Say What Your Strategy Is?', *Harvard Business Review*, April, 82–90.
4. D. J. Collis and M. G. Rukstad (2008) 'Can You Say What Your Strategy Is?', *Harvard Business Review*, April, 82–90.
5. P. Drucker (1964) *Managing for Results*, New York: HarperCollins.
6. Roberts (2004) *The Modern Firm*, Oxford: Oxford University Press, 164–5.
7. T. Obloj and M. Sengul (2012) 'Incentive Life Cycles: Learning and the Division of Value in Firms', *Administrative Science Quarterly*, 57, 305–47.

8. J. R. Galbraith (2009) *Designing Matrix Organizations That Actually Work*, San Francisco: Jossey-Bass.
9. J. B. See Barney (1991) 'Firm Resources and Sustained Competitive Advantage', *Journal of Management*, 17, 99–120; M. Peteraf (1993) 'The Cornerstones of Competitive Advantage: A Resource Based View', *Strategic Management Journal*, 14, 179–91; D. J. Teece, G. Pisano and A. Shuen (1997) 'Dynamic Capabilities and Strategic Management', *Strategic Management Journal*, 18, 509–33.
10. S. Tilles (1963) 'How to Evaluate Corporate Strategy', *Harvard Business Review*, July–August, 111–21.
11. N. Siggielkow (2002) 'Evolution toward Fit', *Administrative Science Quarterly*, 47, 125–59.
12. M. M. Andersen and F. Pulfelt (2006) *Discount Business Strategy*, New York: Wiley.
13. P. Williamson and M. Zeng (2009) 'Value for Money Strategies for Recessionary Times', *Harvard Business Review*, March, 67–74.
14. J. Pfferer (1997) *The Human Equation*, Boston: Harvard Business School Press.
15. J. Roberts (2004) *The Modern Firm*, Oxford: Oxford University Press.
16. M. J. Siverstein and N. Friske (2003) *Trading Up: The New American Luxury*, New York: Penquin Group.
17. Description and analysis is based on N. Siggielkow (2001) 'Change in the Presence of Fit: The Rise, the Fall and the Renaissance of Liz Clairborne', *The Academy of Management Journal*, 44, 838–57; A. J. Mayo and M. Benson (2008) *Liz Clairborne and the New Working Women*, HBS case study 9-407-060.
18. J. Rivkin and N. Siggelkow (2003) 'Balancing Search and Stability: Interdependencies among Elements of Organizational Design', *Organization Science*, 49, 290–311.
19. C. C. Markides and P. A. Geroski (2005) *Fast Second*, New York: Wiley, 1.
20. See http://www.atlas.com.pl/en/grupa/, accessed December 20, 2012.
21. The Atlas story is described by one of the company's founders R. Rojek in his Polish book *Marka narodowa* (National brand), GWP, Gdansk 2007.
22. There is also another reason that became important over time, this is conflict about regulatory issues with Chinese authorities.
23. J. R. Immelt, V. Govindarajan and Ch. Trimble (2009) 'How GE Is Disrupting Itself', *Harvard Business Review*, October, 1–11.
24. J. Roberts (2004) *The Modern Firm*, Oxford: Oxford University Press, 48–9.
25. The experiment was successful, but not accepted on a large scale – neither by managers, nor by trade unions. Finally, in 2009, GM closed this division.
26. This discussion is based upon K. Corts and D. Freier (2002) *Judo in Action*, HBS case study 9-703-454; D. McDonald, Red Bull's Millionaire Maniac, *Business Week*, May 19, 2011, web page http://en.wikipedia.org/wiki/Red_Bull, accessed November 16, 2011 and the company web page: www.red bull.com.
27. The company web page has information regarding the ingredients of the drink.
28. S. Mishkin and S. Pearson (2013) 'Foxconn Faces Culture Clash as Its Global Reach Grows', *Financial Times*, January 4, 13.

7 Company Adrift – Inertia, Organizational Games and Unsure Leaders

1. Inertia is a very extensively studied topic. See: M. W. Meyer and L. G. Zucker (1989) *Permanently Failing Organizations*, Newbury Park: Sage; D. Miller (1990) *The Icarus Paradox: How Exceptional Companies Bring About Their Own Fall*, New York: Harper Collins; Kelly and T. L. Amburgey (1991) 'Organizational Inertia and Momentum: A Dynamic Model of Strategic Change', *Academy of Management Journal*, 34, 591–612.
2. C. K. Prahalad and R. A. Bettis (1986) 'The Dominant Logic: A New Linkage between Diversity and Performance', *Strategic Management Journal*, 7, 485–501; J. P. Walsh (1995) 'Managerial and Organizational Cognition: Notes from a Trip Down Memory Lane', *Organizational Science*, 6, 280–320; T. Obloj, K. Obloj and M. Pratt (2010) 'Dominant Logic and Entrepreneurial Firms Performance in a Transitional Market', *Entrepreneurship: Theory and Practice*, 34, 151–70.
3. W.W. Powell (2000) 'The Sources of Managerial Logics', in J. A. Baum and F. Dobbin, *Economics Meets Sociology in Strategic Management*, Stamford: JAI Press.
4. The analysis is based upon an Mary Tripsas and Giovanni Gavetti (2000) 'Capabilities, Cognition and Inertia: Evidence from Digital Imaging', *Strategic Management Journal*, 21, 1147–61 and http://en.wikipedia.org/wiki/Polaroid_Corporation, accessed November 17, 2012.
5. Mary Tripsas and Giovanni Gavetti (2000) 'Capabilities, Cognition and Inertia: Evidence from Digital Imaging', *Strategic Management Journal*, 21, 1147–61.
6. J. Bogle (2009) *Enough: True Measures of Money, Business, and Life*, New York: Wiley.
7. R. Nelson and S. Winter (1982) *An Evolutionary Theory of Economic Change*, Boston: Harvard University Press; J. G. March (1996) 'Continuity and Change in Theories of Organizational Action', *Administrative Science Quarterly*, 41, 278–87; S. Nadkarni and P. D. Perez (2007) 'Prior Commitments and Early International Commitment: The Mediating Role of Domestic Mindset', *Journal of International Business Studies*, 38, 160–76.
8. I. Nonaka and H. Takeuchi (1995) *The Knowledge Creating Company*, Oxford: Oxford University Press.
9. M. Crozier (1964) *The Bureaucratic Phenomena*, Chicago: Chicago University Press.
10. K. Obloj and P. Joynt (1985) 'An Empirical Study of Innovative Behaviour in Poland' in P. Joynt and M. Warner *Managing in Different Cultures*, Oslo: Universitetsforlaget; A. K. Kozminski and K. Obloj (1983) *Gry o innowacje* (Game for innovations), Warsaw: PWE.
11. R. A. Burgelman and A. S. Grove (2007) 'Let Chaos Reign, then Rein in Chaos – Repeatedly: Managing Strategic Dynamics for Corporate Longevity', *Strategic Management Journal*, 28, 972.
12. R. A. Burgelman and A. S. Grove (2007) 'Let Chaos Reign, then Rein in Chaos – Repeatedly: Managing Strategic Dynamics for Corporate Longevity', *Strategic Management Journal*, 28, 973.

13. A. G. Lafley (2009), 'What only the CEO Can Do', *Harvard Business Review*, May, 56.
14. J. G. March and T. Weil (2005) *On Leadership*, Oxford: Blackwell, 11; M. J. Hatch, M. Kostera and A. K. Kozminski (2005) *The Three Faces of Leadership: Manager, Artist, Priest*, Oxford: Blackwell.
15. J.P. Kotter (2001) 'What Leaders Really Do', *Harvard Business Review*, December, 85–96; J. P. Kotter (1998) *Leadership Factor*, New York: The Free Press.
16. S. Lem (1973) *Invincible*, London: Sidgwick and Jackson.
17. S. Lem (1968) *Solaris. Niezwyciężony, Kraków: Wydawnictwo Literackie*, 323–4 (my own translation).

Index